THE MESSIAH RETURNS

Daniel through Revelation

FRANK PACE

The Messiah Returns

© 2018 Frank Pace

ISBN: 9781731251220

FOREWORD

After an early childhood exposure to Christ, I became a Christian in 1975 at the age of 23. In 1979, I volunteered to teach the high school group at my local church. After finishing a series on the Gospels, I asked the students if there was something they wanted to study next. It was almost unanimous that they wanted to study prophecy and the end times. I told them that I wasn't qualified to teach on that topic. However, their eagerness encouraged me to consider teaching the topic and I told them I would teach the topic after several months of study.

During the next several months I set out to learn about end times prophecy. Since I was a fairly new Christian I did not know much about the topic. When I study a topic thoroughly, I like to reread the Bible and collect all the texts that are significant and then study those texts thoroughly. My then current bias about the end times prophecy was shaped by the position of my church, which was similar to most evangelical churches. That position can be summarized as follows:

1. Christ will return in the air and collect (rapture), the church (Christians).

2. The beast will then preside over a seven-year tribulation.
3. Christ will return to earth to conquer the beast.
4. Christ will rule on earth with Christians for 1,000 years.
5. A new heaven and new earth will then be created.
6. Christians will reign with Christ on the new earth for the rest of eternity.

However, as I read Matthew, Mark, Luke and John, I found very little to support the above outlined timing of the rapture. In fact, the Gospels seemed in conflict with the above timing of the rapture. Intrigued by this discovery, I developed a timeline for the events of the end times and that is what I taught. My position has changed slightly over the years, but at its core, it is the same. In this book I will explain in some detail what I believe is the biblical timing of these endtime events, including the rapture.

TABLE OF CONTENTS

INTRODUCTION

The goal of this book is to create a timeline of endtimes events. I will not attempt to extract the meaning of every eschatological symbol in Scripture, as some things will always be a mystery – but I will attempt to place all events in a chronological order. My main guideline will be to assume if a prophecy is not completely fulfilled then it still must be fulfilled sometime in the future.

In Deuteronomy 18:18-22, the Lord proclaims that if a prophet's words are from God they will come true. If they do not come true, that prophet should die for he has spoken presumptuously. In Jeremiah 1:11-12 the Lord states, "I am watching over My word to perform it." Clearly just as the Lord is serious about prophecy being fulfilled, we should be too!

The Study

Of course, there are many ways to approach this study. One way is to dive right into the book of Revelation, but that would be like reading the last chapter of a book and hoping to gain an understanding of the entire book. I believe the best way is to start in the book of Daniel, because Daniel gives an overall framework of the end-times upon which all other end-times details should be placed. Another reason to start with Daniel is because that is the order that God revealed these prophecies. It is important to remember that God has given man incremental bits of knowledge through time. Each new item of information builds on the foundation that God laid before it. Therefore, this book will address the relevant end-times texts in the order in which they were written.

An exhaustive study would, of course, include many more texts than I will include here. But in order to narrow down the study, I will cover the following:

1. Daniel 2
2. Daniel 7
3. Daniel 9
4. Daniel 10,11 & 12
5. Matthew 24
6. 1 Thessalonians 4:13-18
7. 2 Thessalonians 1:6-8
8. 2 Thessalonians 2:1-12
9. Revelation 1-22

The above texts have been chosen because they are direct teachings on the end-times and not just an aside mention of a concept. It is assumed that this book will be read with the Bible open (either in paper form or electronically), because each passage and verse is not always given verbatim in this book. One final note: the study is based on the New American Standard Bible, so it might be handy to have that version available so it can be referenced if there is confusion.

Definitions

For those unfamiliar with end times jargon, here are some simple definitions for key words and phrases that will be used throughout this book.

- **Jesus Christ's second coming** – One thing that all believers can agree upon is that Christ is coming again. We do not know when but we know with certainty that he is coming again (John 14:2-3).

- **End-times** - The time immediately preceding and immediately following Christ's second coming. When this period will begin is the age old question.

- **The Tribulation** – In life, trials can occur at any time and often do, but The Tribulation in our context will be the last seven years before Christ physically rules on earth. The Tribulation is a time of great distress in the world. I will capitalize the words "The Tribulation" in this book to make it clear that I am referring to the seven years before Christ physically rules on earth.

- **Daniel's 70th week** -The same seven year period as The Tribulation

- **The beast** – A real person, also known as the antichrist, who is empowered by Satan and rules over nearly all of the earth during The Tribulation

- **Rapture** – The gathering up and the removing of living Christians from the earth to be with the Lord in heaven. Just prior to the rapture Christians who have passed away will be raised. (1 Thess 4:16-17).

- **Millennium** – A thousand year period of Christ's rule on earth after his second coming. The literal fulfillment of this time period is a position held by many Christians.

- **Amillennial** – A theological position that maintains the millennial kingdom is not literal and generally maintains that Christ is ruling on earth now through the church.

- **Imminent return of Christ** – A theological position asserting that Christ could return at any time to rapture His church. This is a position held by many Christians.

Overall Prophecy Viewpoints

There are several overall viewpoints on prophecy that are maintained by Christians. The four main beliefs are:

Preterist	Preterists believe that most proph-ecies about the end-times were fulfilled by the fall of Jerusalem in 70 AD. (This is an amillenial position.)
Idealist	Idealists believe that Revelation is a theological poem depicting the timeless struggle between the kingdom of light and the kingdom of darkness. It speaks with allegories and symbols; it does not refer to actual historical events. (This is an amillennial position.)

Historicist	Historicists believe that Revelation, especially Revelation 4:1 – 20:6, is a forecast of the events that will occur between the birth of the church (Acts 2) and return of Christ. Historicists see in Revelation the history of western Europe, various popes, the Protestant Reformation, the French Revolution, Charlemagne, Mussolini, etc. (This is an amillennial position.)
Futurist	Futurists believe that Revelation 4-22 is about a future period of history. It pertains primarily to events surrounding Christ's second coming. This position generally believes in a literal 1,000 year rule by Christ on earth after his second coming.

This book is written from the futurist point of view and assumes that there is a literal 1,000 year period when Christ rules physically on earth. The reason for taking this position will be discussed in the book, but to state it briefly, I believe that all prophecy must be completely fulfilled or it is not true prophecy (Deut 18:18-22). Even a quick reading of Revelation leads to the conclusion that many prophecies have not yet been fulfilled, therefore the fulfillment must occur at some point in the future. For example, the trumpets of Revelation 8 do not have any fulfillment in documented history. At the first trumpet, fire comes down from heaven and burns up a third of the earth. The ministry and the resurrection of the two witnesses in Revelation 11 has not happened, nor the necessity of the mark of the beast to conduct trade as described in Revelation 13. Daniel 7:27 states that all dominions on earth are following Christ, and clearly that has not come true yet.

You might be thinking "if it is so obvious that the prophecies have not been fulfilled then why isn't everybody a futurist?" The main reason that some people do not hold the futurist interpretation is because there are many references in the Bible that declare that Christ's return is near. For example,

"You too be patient; strengthen your hearts, for the coming of the Lord is near. Do not complain, brethren, against one another, so that you yourselves may not be judged; behold, the Judge is standing right at the door." (James 5:8-9).

"The end of all things is near; therefore, be of sound judgment and sober spirit for the purpose of prayer (1 Pet 4:7).

See also Romans 13:11-12, 16:20, Hebrews 10:36-37, 1 John 4:3, Revelation 1:3, 22:12, 22:20.

The preterist uses these verses to support the position that Christ came back in 70 AD. Admittedly the futurist needs to resolve the problem with the many passages stating or implying that the return of Christ is near. However, the problem can not be solved by saying that Christ has already returned. Jesus' teaching in Matthew 24:27-30 says his (Christ's) return will be dramatic and not go unnoticed, which clearly has not happened.

My solution to the "nearness" problem is threefold:

1. None of the writers knew when Christ was returning, but were inspired by the Spirit to write as if His return was near to be consistent with God's perspective.
2. One thousand years is like a day to God (2 Pet 3:8). Therefore, what is near to God does not seem near to us.
3. Looking at it individually, Christ's return is near because when we die our souls go to heaven but our bodies sleep until Christ's return. Our death is always near; it can happen at any time.

Rapture Viewpoints

A fair amount of this book will discuss issues that relate to the timing of the rapture. This is the event foretold in the Bible in which Christ returns and gathers up believers to be with Him. The most popular description of this event occurs in Thessalonians.

"For the Lord Himself will descend from heaven with a shout, with the voice of the archangel and with the trumpet of God, and the dead in Christ will rise first. Then we who are alive and remain will be caught up together with them in the clouds to meet the Lord in the air, and so we shall always be with the Lord."
(1 Thess 4:16-17)

One of the great debates among futurist Christians is about the timing of the rapture. When does this rapture occur? Unfortunately one's position on this topic has divided Christians who, otherwise, might be in perfect doctrinal agreement on all other issues. The dominant belief of the futurist believers is the pre-tribulation rapture position. This position holds that the rapture occurs right before The Tribulation (the 7 year period). Some churches do not want any other position discussed, and some churches have even gone so far as to make belief in the pre-trib rapture a membership requirement. Some other churches will not allow discussion about a position different from the pre-trib rapture. In my opinion, failing to allow biblical discussion on any topic is damaging to the church. Christians should always be allowed to verify what they are being taught by comparing it to the Bible just as the Bereans did in Acts 17:10-11.

The most popular rapture timing positions are as follows:

Pre-tribulation (Pre-trib)	The rapture occurs before the start of the final 7 years of The Tribulation. This position is based on the promise in the Bible that Christians are not destined for the wrath of God (1 Thess 5:9), and that Christ could return at any moment to gather his church. For Christ to return at any moment (imminent) it must be before the start of The Tribulation.
Mid-tribulation (Mid-trib)	The rapture occurs at the midpoint of The Tribulation. This is the moment Satan is thrown out of heaven down to earth (Rev 12:7-10) and therefore must be when God's wrath is poured out.

Pre-wrath	The rapture occurs in the last part of The Tribulation. Agreeing with the pre-trib position that Christians are not destined for wrath, this position holds that God's wrath does not occur until fairly late in The Tribulation, typically after the sixth seal (Rev 6:12-17)
Post-tribulation (Post-trib)	The rapture occurs at the end of The Tribulation . Christ only comes once to gather his elect and vanquish Satan at the same time. (2 Thess 1:6-8)

I believe that the description of events, given by Christ in Matthew 24:29-31, is a description of the rapture.

"But immediately after the tribulation of those days THE SUN WILL BE DARKENED, AND THE MOON WILL NOT GIVE ITS LIGHT, AND THE STARS WILL FALL from the sky, and the powers of heaven will be shaken. "And then the sign of the Son of Man will appear in the sky, and then all the tribes of the earth will mourn, and they will see the SON OF MAN COMING ON THE CLOUDS OF THE SKY with power and great glory. "And He will send forth His angels with A GREAT TRUMPET and THEY WILL GATHER TOGETHER His elect from the four winds, from one end of the sky to the other." (Matt 24:29-31)

The timing of this passage is a major discussion in this book.

DANIEL 2

In Daniel 2, king Nebuchadnezzar had a dream that he wanted interpreted. Being clever, and wanting a true interpretation, he refused to tell the wise men, magicians, enchanters, sorcerers and astrologers his dream. Most likely Nebuchadnezzar reasoned that he usually received a made-up interpretation. Thus, his plan required a supernatural revelation of the dream to the interpreter and therefore, the interpretation would be trustworthy. Being firm in his plan he said that if no one came forward with the dream and its interpretation, all the magicians, enchanters, sorcerers and astrologers would be put to death. When Daniel heard the king's words, he asked for time and promised to reveal the dream and the interpretation. To the king's surprise, God revealed both to Daniel.

The dream was of a giant statue.

- The head of the statue was made of pure gold.
- Its chest and arms were of silver.
- Its belly and thighs were of bronze.
- Its legs were of iron.

- Its feet were partly of iron and partly of baked clay.
- The statue was crushed on the feet by a rock not made from human hands.

Daniel's interpretation of the dream revealed that the statue represented future kingdoms. The head represented the present time, and the future unfolded going down the statue ending with the feet and finally the toes. As stated in the text, the gold head represents Nebuchadnezzar and Babylon. A common belief among many biblical scholars and historians is that:

- The chest and arms of silver represent Media/Persia.
- The belly and thighs of bronze represent Greece.
- The legs of iron represent Rome.
- The feet partly of clay and partly of iron represent a divided kingdom.
- The ten toes are ten future kings.

In the days of the ten toes (the final part of kingdom history as time runs from head to toe), God will set up a kingdom that will endure forever (Dan 2:44). This kingdom will take over the whole earth and is commonly equated with Christ's return and reign. The ten toes are commonly believed to be the ten kings mentioned in Daniel 7 and Revelation 17. These ten kings will be discussed later.

To summarize:

Head	Babylon 605 BC to 562 BC
Chest and Arms	Media/Persia 550 BC to 330 BC
Belly and Thighs	Greece 332 BC to 323 BC Divides into 4 parts until 146 BC
Legs	Rome Republic 146 BC to 27 BC Roman Empire until 476 AD
Feet	A divided kingdom some parts will be strong others weak
Ten Toes	Ten future kings, but part of the divided kingdom represented by the feet. During this period the kingdom that will last forever is established.

The important part of Daniel 2, for understanding the end-times, is that God will create a final kingdom that will last forever at the time of the ten toes.

"In the days of those kings the God of heaven will set up a kingdom which will never be destroyed , and that kingdom will not be left for another people; it will crush and put an end to all these kingdoms, but it will itself endure forever." (Dan 2:44)

The Roman kingdom transitions from legs of iron (very strong) to feet of iron and clay (a much weaker situation) to fragile toes partly of iron and partly of clay. The situation at the time of the ten toes is described as follows:

> "As the toes of the feet were partly of iron and partly of pottery, so some of the kingdom will be strong and part of it will be brittle." (Dan 2:42).

The next verse states that the parts of the kingdom will not adhere strongly to each other.

> "And in that you saw the iron mixed with common clay, they will combine with one another in the seed of men; but they will not adhere to one another, even as iron does not combine with pottery." (Dan 2:43)

Christ will return and establish his kingdom at the time of ten kings (ten toes) who are in some way descended from the Roman empire. These ten kings are mentioned again in Daniel 7 and Revelation 17. Thus, the ten kings are not a one-time occurrence based on an interpretation of the ten toes. (Currently Europe is a loosely connected set of countries, some of which are strong and some are weak. Most likely ten of these countries will combine in some way to become the ten toe descendant of the Roman Empire.)

Implications from Daniel 2 are:
A. Precludes Preterists' beliefs.

In 70 AD the Roman kingdom was very strong; it was not divided into weak and strong parts. This known history precludes the Preterists' belief that Christ's kingdom was set up and that nearly all prophesy was fulfilled by 70 AD. Christ's everlasting kingdom is set up at the time of the ten toes, and his everlasting kingdom crushes all other kingdoms. Clearly, this has not happened yet.

B. Precludes Christ's imminent return.

Many Christians believe that the Bible teaches the imminent return of Christ, i.e. that Christ can return at any time. When the Bible was being written, Rome was a strong, united kingdom (legs of iron). The prophet Daniel made it clear that Christ would not return to set up his kingdom until the time of the ten toes. Hence, Christ's return was not imminent in the first century when the Scripture was being written. Therefore, the Bible does not teach the imminent return of Christ, but rather that his kingdom is established after the ten kings are established.

DANIEL 7

In Daniel 7, the Prophet Daniel sees a vision of four beasts. The first three are equated to an animal, but the last one is not except that it has ten horns.

1. Lion
2. Bear
3. Leopard with four heads
4. Terrifying beast with ten horns

The common interpretation of these beasts is that they are the same kingdoms represented in the statue of Daniel chapter 2. Thus,

1. The lion represents Babylon
2. The bear represents Media Persia
3. The leopard represents Greece. Its four heads represent the four separate kings that come out of the Greek empire.
4. The last beast is not compared to an earthly beast or animal. It is portrayed as dreadful, terrifying and extremely strong representing the Roman Empire.

TIMELINE 1 on the following page presents the timeline for the kings of Daniel 2 and Daniel 7.

The last beast is said to have ten horns and an additional horn arises (Dan 7:8). These ten horns and the additional horn are explained in 7:24, so there is no need to speculate on their meaning. The ten horns are ten kings.

"As for the ten horns, out of this kingdom ten kings will arise; and another will arise after them, and he will be different from the previous ones and will subdue three kings." (Dan 7:24)

One additional king conquers three of the ten kings.

"While I was contemplating the horns, behold, another horn, a little one, came up among them, and three of the first horns were pulled out by the roots before it; and behold, this horn possessed eyes like the eyes of a man and a mouth uttering great boasts." (Dan. 7:8)

These ten kings are also represented by the ten toes of the statue in Daniel 2:41-42. The ten kings are also mentioned in Revelation 17:3, 7, 12, and 16.

In Daniel 2:44, at the time of the ten kings, the everlasting kingdom will be set up without human hands and all the earthly kingdoms will disappear. Also in Daniel 7, it is important to notice that there is another king, a little one, that arises (Dan 7:8). Although this king is "little" he conquers 3 kings. Daniel 2 describes some of these kings as weak and some as strong. The once "little" king is soon uttering great boasts and becomes larger in appearance than the other kings (Dan 7:20).

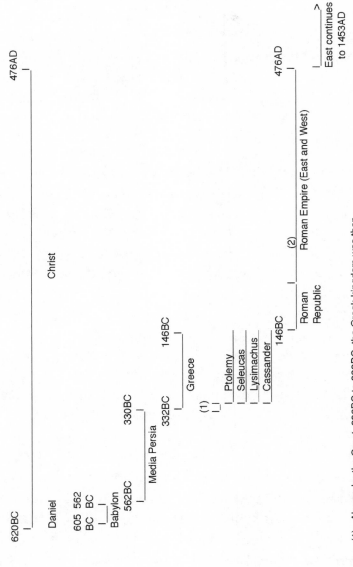

TIMELINE 1 - KINGDOM TIMELINE FOR DANIEL 2 & 7

(1) - Alexander the Great, 332BC to 323BC, the Greek kingdom was then split into four kingdoms

(2) - Rome destroys Jerusalem in 70AD

In Daniel 7:9,10, 13 and 14 the vision breaks away from the earthly scene to show what is happening in the heavenly realm at this time. In this heavenly description, God the Father is called the "Ancient of Days" (Dan 7:9, 13) and Jesus is called the "Son of Man" (Dan 7:13). Later in the chapter Jesus is called "the Highest One" (Dan 25,27). As Daniel is watching, thrones are being set up for a court to convene and pass judgment. Revelation 4 and 5 describe the same scene. Revelation 4 gives a depiction of 24 thrones.

However, in Daniel 7 the focus is on the throne of God, the Ancient of Days. After this incredible description of God, it states, "the court sat in judgement and the books were opened" (Dan 7:10). No further information about "the books" (Dan 7:10) are given in Daniel 7, but it seems "the books" contained information needed for the court. The likely books are mentioned in Revelation 20:12.

"And I saw the dead, the great and the small,
standing before the throne, and books were opened;
and another book was opened, which is the book of
life; and the dead were judged from the things, which
were written in the books, according to their deeds"
(Rev 20:12).

The books of deeds record the good and bad things which people have done. Deeds cannot get anyone into heaven. People only go to heaven if their names are written in the book of life. (The book of life will be covered in detail in the discussion of Revelation 5 and 6). After the books are opened the verdict of the court is to destroy the beast and take away its dominion and the dominion from all the other beasts (Dan 7:11-12)

At this time, the Son of Man (Christ) appears in the heavenly clouds (Dan. 7:13) and is given dominion, glory and a kingdom, which will not pass away or be destroyed (Dan. 7:14). The same kingdom is referenced in Daniel 2:44.

Fortunately, Daniel was distressed by the vision and asked for the true interpretation of the vision (Dan 7:15-16). It is always best when the Bible interprets itself, removing all speculation and doubt. The first interpretation given in Daniel 7:17-18 is amazingly brief, encapsulating at least 2700 years of earthly history. In summary, the interpretation is that there will be some kingdoms, but in the end Christ and his saints will receive the kingdom and possess it forever. Perhaps Christians should view history and their lives in such a way, i.e. Believers will live their lives on earth and do some things but in the end, they will possess the kingdom with Christ forever, and that is what matters. This truth should change believers' daily perspective on life. Perhaps Christians would focus more on their name being written in the book of life and on serving Christ.

Daniel was not satisfied with the short answer given in Daniel 7:17-18, but wanted to know more about the final terrifying beast, the 10 horns, and the additional horn (Dan 7:19-22). Daniel adds a very key fact as he is pressing for more information. The key fact is that this small, turned to large, horn is waging war with the saints of the Highest One (Jesus Christ) and he is overpowering them (Dan 7:21).

Daniel 7:23-27 is the expanded explanation of verses 17 and 18. Apparently, this being standing near was not one for long conversations, so there is a limited explanation to Daniel's question. The sequence given is as follows:

1. A terrifying final earthly kingdom will arise (Rome).
2. Ten kings will arise out of that kingdom.
3. Another king will arise who will subdue 3 kings.
4. He will be opposed to Christ and Christians.
5. He will want to change times and laws.
6. Christians will be in his hand for a time, times and half a time.
7. The heavenly court will sit for judgment.
8. The oppressing king's dominion is taken away and destroyed forever.
9. The dominion of all kingdoms is given to Christ and his saints.
10. All dominions serve and obey Christ.

A few comments regarding this sequence are necessary:

First, the ten kings have not yet come. Daniel 2 states that at the time of these kings Christ's everlasting kingdom will be set up. Some Christians believe that Christ's kingdom is already set up and Christians are already reigning (Preterist position). A problem with this position is that worldly dominions are not serving and obeying Christ (contrary to item 10 on the above list). The Preterist position holds that Christ's kingdom was set up in 70 AD. This contradicts Daniel 2, which describes a clay-mixed-with-iron divided kingdom that is partially weak prior to the ten toes (kingdoms). Rome was not partially weak in 70 AD.

There are many candidates for the ten kings descended from the Roman kingdom. At one time the ten kings were thought to be the European Union (EU). The EU has grown to over 20 countries but it is interesting to note that it has started to fracture with the UK voting to pull out in June of 2016. The EU may eventually be the ten kings; however, it could be some other treaty or agreement that combines ten kings. These ten kings may only be apparent when the time comes.

Second, this small-to-large horn is the beast of Revelation. This will become clear in the next several chapters. The beast wages war against Christians, he overpowers (Dan 7:21) and wears down (7:25) the saints of the Highest One (Christ).

The time period of a time, times, and half a time is a poetic way of saying three and a half years (same phrase in Dan 7:25 and 12:7). In Revelation 12, two ways of saying 3.5 years are mentioned.

1. "Then the woman fled into the wilderness where she had a place prepared by God, so that there she would be nourished for one thousand two hundred and sixty days" (Rev 12:6)
2. "But the two wings of the great eagle were given to the woman, so that she could fly into the wilderness to her place, where she was nourished for a time and times and half a time, from the presence of the serpent" (Rev 12:14).

Note: Prophetic years are based on the Jewish calendar, which has 360 days, so 3.5 years is 42 months. 42 months x 30 days = 1260 days.

Daniel 7:18, 27 are the first verses in the Bible that promise the saints will rule with Christ over the earth once the beast is eliminated. These verses support a literal 1,000 year reign of Christ on earth (Millennium) after the beast is destroyed.

In summary, the sequence of Daniel 7 is as follows:

1. Kingdom 1 – Babylon: Lion with wings of eagle.
   (Dan 7:4)
2. Kingdom 2 – Media-Persia: Bear. (Dan 7:5)
3. Kingdom 3 – Greece: Leopard. (Dan 7:6)
4. Kingdom 4 – Rome: Dreadful and terrifying. (Dan 7:7,8)
   a. Transforms eventually into ten kingdoms,
      ten horns.
   b. Final Kingdom - Beast, little horn.
   c. Little horn (beast) conquers three kings.
   d. The beast utters great boasts.
5. Thrones in heaven set up for judgment. (Dan 7:9)
6. God takes his seat. (Dan 7:9)
7. Books are opened. (Dan 7:10)
8. The beast wears down the saints for 3.5 years.
   (Dan 7:25)
9. The beast is slain, and given to burning fire. (Dan 7:11)
10. Jesus, the Son of Man = the Highest One, is given an
    eternal kingdom. (Dan 7:13,14)
11. The saints rule with Jesus. (Dan 7:27)

TIMELINE 2 on the following page provides a time line of this sequence combined with facts from Daniel 2.

TIMELINE 2 - DANIEL CHAPTER 2 & 7 TIMELINE OF FUTURE THINGS

(1)(2)(3)

(4)(5)

(6)

The books are opened to be reviewed by the court, one has seven seals (Dan. 7:10,Rev 5:1)

The beast is very boastful (Dan. 7:8,11)

For 3.5 years the beast shatters the power of the saints (Dan.7:21,25)

Everlasting kingdom with Christ and saints ruling (Dan. 2:44, 7:18, 22, 27)

(1) - Ten kings arise out of Rome, some strong, some brittle, Daniel 2:42, 7:24

(2) - Little horn (beast) arises, Daniel 7:8,24

(3) - Beast conquers 3 kings, Dan 7:8

(4) - Thrones are set up in preparation for judgment court, Daniel 7:9

(5) - Heavenly court sits for judgment, Daniel 7:10,26

(6) - Beast thrown into the lake of fire, Daniel 7:11,9:27, Revelation 19:20

DANIEL 9

In this study, Daniel 9 is the third of four prophetic passages in Daniel to examine. It is interesting to note that Daniel time-stamps each of these chapters with who the king is and the year of their reign. Since Daniel gives time markers, the years between prophecies can easily be calculated. After the vision given in Daniel 2, Daniel waits 51 years to get the more detailed account in Daniel 7.

Daniel 2	604 BC
Daniel 7	553 BC
Daniel 9	538 BC
Daniel 11-12	536 BC

Daniel waits another 15 years after the vision of Daniel 7 before he has the vision described in Daniel 9. Daniel 9 begins with Daniel praying, noting that God had said that the length of the Jewish exile to Babylon will last 70 years. Daniel clearly believed that God would keep his prophetic word and soon the Jews would return to Jerusalem. The key part of Daniel 9 for this study is the end (Dan 9:24-27), where the angel Gabriel gives a brief prophetic utterance.

In many ways Daniel 9:24-27 is a key passage for discussing The Tribulation period. It is the only passage, in the Bible, that mentions a time period of seven years, which is the commonly held view regarding the length of The Tribulation. Daniel 9:27 also states that the midpoint of the seven years is a critical time and includes the concept of a prince (beast) who is to come.

Before the future implications of Daniel 9 are considered, it is worthwhile to look at all of Daniel 9:24-27 and the timing for the Messiah's first coming.

The prophecy states that 70 weeks are decreed for the Jewish people. The literal meaning of the word for week is "seven". So the passage indicates that there are 70 sevens. Most Christians believe that these sevens are periods of years, and the timing of the Messiah's first coming confirms this belief.

The decree to rebuild Jerusalem is discussed in Nehemiah 2:1-5. Nehemiah 2:1 indicates that the decree was given in the 20th year of Artaxerxes reign, which according to most scholars was 445 BC. Daniel 9:25 states that it will be 69 sevens (483 years) until Messiah the prince arrives. To get the exact year, convert the 483 prophetic years commonly thought to be 360 days each to our 365 day calendar. Hence,

$$445BC + 483 * (360/365) = 32 \text{ AD}.$$

When adjustment is made for leap years, many say that the equation calculates exactly to Palm Sunday. Whether that is true, I do not know, but it is, none the less, an extremely accurate marker for the time of the Messiah. This incredible prophecy can be a witnessing tool with Jewish friends if they are open to it, because these texts are the same in their Scripture.

TIMELINE 3 summarizes the timing of Daniel's 70 weeks.

TIMELINE 3 - DANIEL'S 70 WEEKS, DANIEL 9:24-27

445BC

7 weeks

62 weeks

32AD*

|------GAP------|

70AD

(1) (2)

(3)
(4)
(5)
(6)

* The calculation is 69 weeks * 7 yrs * 360 days/365 days = 476.4 years

GAP - an undetermined amount of time between the first 69 weeks and the final week (7 years)

(1) - Messiah the Prince is cut off and has nothing, Daniel 9:26
(2) - People of the prince (beast) destroy Jerusalem, Daniel 9:26
(3) - Daniel's 70th week = to 7 years, Daniel 9:27
(4) - Firm covenant signed between the beast and many start the last 7 years, Daniel 9:27
(5) - Sacrifice is stopped by the beast in the middle of the week, Daniel 9:27
(6) - Beast thrown into the lake of fire, Daniel 7:11,9:27, Revelation 19:20

The important element of this text (Dan. 9:24-27), for the discussion in this book, relates to the final seven year period. The passage states that there will be 70 sevens, but only 69 sevens until the Messiah. Daniel 9:25-26 states, after the 7 sevens and 62 sevens, the Messiah will be cut off and have nothing. This refers, of course, to the crucifixion. After the Messiah is cut off there is still one more seven year period. The common belief among futurist Christians is that the final seven years has not happened yet. The final seven years is believed to occur right before Christ returns again to reign on earth. This period is commonly called The Tribulation.

This position demands a gap between the 69th seven and the last seven. The text does seem to imply the gap by the delay in fulfillment of one more incredibly accurate prophesy. In Daniel 9:26, it predicts the people of a prince who is to come will destroy Jerusalem and the sanctuary. Jerusalem was destroyed by Rome in 70 AD which is a significant gap from Christ's death and resurrection. In 9:27 the additional prince, who is to come, makes a covenant that is to last seven years. This covenant period is the final seven years. This is often referred to as the 70th week of Daniel. This final seven year period starts at some point after the destruction of Jerusalem (70 AD) demanding a gap between the 69th and the 70th seven.

Another argument for the gap between the 69th seven and the last seven is that Daniel 9:24 says that the seventy sevens will:

1. Finish the transgression,
2. Make an end of sin,
3. Make atonement for iniquity,
4. Bring in everlasting righteousness,

5. Seal up vision and prophecy and

6. Anoint the most holy place.

Most would agree that the above list has not been completed. For example, the end of the transgression or the end of sin has obviously not happened! Also, the everlasting righteousness has not happened (probably a reference to the final everlasting kingdom discussed in Daniel 2:44 and Daniel 7:14,18, and 27). The preterist position holds that the above list is already fulfilled. As mentioned in the introduction, this book assumes the futurist position, which would hold that the above list is not fulfilled yet.

Looking again at Daniel 9:26-27 it is unfortunately stated that there will be war and desolations to the end.

> "Then after the sixty-two weeks the Messiah will be cut off and have nothing, and the people of the prince who is to come will destroy the city and the sanctuary. And its end will come with a flood; even to the end there will be war; desolations are determined" (Dan 9:26)

Daniel predicts there will be war and desolation to the end contradicting the glorious idea that "civilization will advance to the point that there will be no more war."

In verse 27, the prince (beast) who is to come will set up a covenant with "many" for a seven year period. This covenant period is the final seven years, known as the seventieth week of Daniel and commonly called The Tribulation. In the middle of this week (seven years) this prince, whom the world goes after, will abandon this covenant and put a stop to the sacrifices and offerings in the temple and set up an abomination in the temple.

"And he will make a firm covenant with the many for
one week, but in the middle of the week he will put a
stop to sacrifice and grain offering; and on the wing
of abominations will come one who makes desolate,
even until a complete destruction, one that is decreed,
is poured out on the one who makes desolate."
(Dan. 9:27)

This prince (beast) will cause desolation until his destruction. The destruction of the beast is first mentioned in Daniel 7:11. The destruction of the beast will take place after he wears down the power of the saints for three and a half years as described in Daniel 7:21,25. Daniel 9:27 also indicates that the beast will put a stop to sacrifice and the grain offering. For these sacrifices to be lawful they must be occurring in the temple. Therefore, it is believed that the temple in Jerusalem must be rebuilt by the midpoint of the final seven year period (The Tribulation).

TIMELINE 4 summarizes the future events discussed so far in Daniel.

TIMELINE 4 - DANIEL CHAPTER 2, 7 & 9 TIMELINE OF FUTURE THINGS

Daniel's 70th week = 7 years

(1)(2)(3)(4)
(5)(6)
(7)
(8)

The books are opened to be reviewed by the court, one has seven seals (Dan. 7:10, Rev 5:1)

The beast is very boastful (Dan. 7:8,11)

For 3.5 years the beast shatters the power of the saints (Dan.7:21,25)

Everlasting kingdom with Christ and saints ruling (Dan. 2:44, 7:18, 22, 27)

(1) - Ten kings arise out of Rome, some strong, some brittle, Daniel 2:42, 7:24
(2) - Little horn (beast) arises, Daniel 7:8,24
(3) - Beast conquers 3 kings, Dan 7:8
(4) - Firm covenant is signed between the beast and many for 7 years, starts Daniel's 70th week, Daniel 9:27
(5) - Thrones are set up in preparation for judgment court, Daniel 7:9
(6) - Heavenly court sits for judgment, Daniel 7:10,26
(7) - Sacrifice stopped, temple abomination of desolation, Daniel 9:27
(8) - Beast thrown into the lake of fire, Daniel 7:11,9:27, Revelation 19:20

DANIEL 10, 11, AND 12

The next part of this study will focus on Daniel 10-12. The prophecy does not start until chapter 11 but the introduction at the start of chapter 10 is quite interesting. After Daniel has been mourning for three weeks, a mighty angel appears. Only Daniel can see the angel; those with him are terrified and run away. The angel had been delayed in coming to him due to an angelic conflict (Dan 10:13). This is a brief glimpse into powers in the heavenlies, something rarely thought about. It is mentioned here in Daniel 10 and Ephesians 6:12-13. The angel then gives Daniel a description of what must take place regarding his people in the latter (final) days (Dan 10:14).

The description is given in Daniel 11 and 12. These chapters provide a consecutive account of major battles that will take place. There is some debate as to when Daniel starts the description of the beast and the end-times. The key marker is Daniel 11:31.

"Forces from him will arise, desecrate the sanctuary fortress, and do away with the regular sacrifice. And they will set up the abomination of desolation."
(Dan 11:31)

Some believe this is a reference to Antiochus IV Epiphanes, a Greek ruler who temporarily took control of the temple in Jerusalem in 165 BC. The rational behind this thought is the earlier verses being a match to battles that Antiochus fought. However, there are many problems with this position. The major one being that Jesus does not agree with it. In Matthew 24:15, Jesus is discussing signs of future things and says to his disciples,

> "Therefore when you see the abomination of desolation which was spoken of through Daniel the prophet, standing in the holy place (let the reader understand), then those who are in Judea must flee to the mountains." (Matt 24:15-16)

Since this is a warning from Jesus to his disciples, the "abomination of desolation" that Jesus envisions must be a future event, not one that occurred almost 200 years prior. Therefore, the verse (Dan.11:31) is not completely fulfilled by Antiochus IV Epiphanes. He is at most a type of the future beast or a partial fulfillment of prophecy.

A difficult question to answer in this prophecy is, "at what point in Daniel 11 does the prophet begin to speak about events that relate to the end times and the beast?" Although I can't say with certainty, I believe that the answer is Daniel 11:22. The "prince of the covenant" (11:22) is most likely a reference to the beast who makes a firm covenant with the many for one week, but in the middle of the week makes an abomination in the temple and stops the sacrifice and grain offerings (Dan. 9:27). The events described from Daniel 11:22-31 seem to unfold sequentially. A logical conclusion is that all events from Daniel 11:22 are future and involve the beast (prince of the covenant). Considering that to be true, some things can be learned about the beast.

According to Daniel 11:21, in a time of tranquility, a despicable person (not the beast) will seize the kingdom by intrigue.

> "In his place a despicable person will arise, on whom the honor of kingship has not been conferred, but he will come in a time of tranquility and seize the kingdom by intrigue." (Dan 11:21)

The sequence of events is then described as follows:

- This despicable person will rise to power. He will slip in and take over the kingdom by flattery and intrigue (Dan 11:21).
- The despicable person will defeat a great army and also defeat the covenant prince (beast) first described in Daniel 9:27 (Dan 11:22).
- The despicable person and the covenant prince (beast) will make an alliance (Dan 11:23).
- The prince of the covenant (beast) and his small army will gain power and wealth, distributing the plunder among his followers (Dan 11:23, 24).
- The prince of the covenant will oppose the king of the south. They will sit at the same table and speak lies (Dan 11:27). This may be a treaty and the signing of the holy covenant which starts The Tribulation (the final seven years).

At some point the beast (prince of the covenant) begins to lose some battles. For whatever reason he becomes enraged about the holy covenant and shows regard for those who break it (11:30). At this point his forces do away with the regular sacrifice and set up the abomination of desolation that Jesus warns about in Matthew 24:15. This event marks the midpoint of the seven years in Daniel 9:27. Daniel 12:7 agrees that the abomination of desolation is the midpoint of the seven years which refers to the three and half years as a time, times and half a time. Daniel 12:11 also agrees and adds an extra 30 days and says there are 1290 days. From this midpoint the beast is turning anyone who forsakes the covenant to godlessness (verse 32).

Daniel 11:33-35 describes a spiritual and physical battle that will take place in which many Christians will be persecuted. These three verses are not clear, however it seems that a group of people with insight (likely Christians) are trying to convince others to the truth of God's word but their efforts have marginal success. During this time, any who oppose the beast are faced with persecution unto death.

Next, in Daniel 11:36 the king (beast/prince of the covenant) will do as he pleases, exalting himself above every god and speaking against the one true God. He abandons the gods of his fathers, has no regard for women, and magnifies himself above all (Dan 11:37). He takes action against the strongest of fortresses (Dan 11:39, also see Rev.17:16). He redistributes land to his supporters who now rule over the people (Dan 11:39). The kings of the North and South oppose him, but he is still victorious over many countries (Dan 11:40). Interestingly Edom, Moab, and part of Ammon (modern day Jordan) are not under his control (Dan 11:41). This must be the mountainous location that Jesus is telling those in Judea to flee to (Matt 24:15-16). The beast takes control of northern Africa (Egypt and Libya and Ethiopia – Dan.11:42-43). Then rumors from the North bother him and he goes forth and annihilates many setting his tents between the seas and the holy mountain (Dan 11:44-45, likely referring to the Mediterranean Sea and where Christ was crucified). The exact details of who the king of the North and the king of the South represent is unknown, but will be clear as the prophecy is being fulfilled.

In Daniel 12:1-2, the angel Michael arises. At this point, Daniel is told that his people will be rescued, and the righteous who sleep (are dead) will be resurrected to everlasting life. Others will be left for everlasting contempt. The group that will be rescued is everyone found written in the book. The book being referred to is almost assuredly the Book of Life (the study of Revelation 4 and 5 will cover this in some detail). One might wonder if this is just referring to the Jews since it refers to Daniel's people. The most logical conclusion is that it is referring to the rapture and resurrection of believers (in which believing Jews participate) as described in 1 Thessalonians 4:13-17. There are two main reasons for this conclusion;

1. The book (of life) is not limited to Jews but contains all those who are to be saved.
2. The raising of the dead which precedes the rapture is a single event and covers all those in the book of life.

This sequence places the rapture well beyond the midpoint of The Tribulation indicated by Daniel 11:31. The study in this book will cover many texts that support this timing.

Next, Daniel is told to conceal these words and seal up the book until the end of time (Dan. 12:4). The book which is to be sealed in the context of this passage is logically the book of life which will appear again in Revelation 5 as a sealed book. Some people believe it is referring to the meaning of the book of Daniel but that does not fit the context.

There is a little prophetic phrase at the end of Daniel 12:4: "many will go back and forth, and knowledge will increase." This has been fulfilled in the last few hundred years as the automobile and the jet age have allowed unprecedented travel. Worldwide in 2017 there were four billion airline passengers. Furthermore, first the printing press, and eventually the internet have caused an explosion of knowledge for the average person. The world-wide literacy rate went from 12% two hundred years ago to over 80% now. As another measure of knowledge, from 1776 to 1870 (nearly 100 years) there were 100,000 patents filed with the US patent office. In 2009 there were 158,000 patents filed in a single year. Christ could not return until these prophetic verses were fulfilled. These prophecies alone indicate that Christ's return was not imminent when the Bible was written.

In Daniel 12:7, the length of time for these events is stated along with the statement that they will be completed when the power of the holy people is shattered. The reference to times, time and half a time (Dan 12:7) and persecution of the holy people (Christians) is exactly the same as in Daniel 7:21, 25. Then Daniel asks what is the outcome of this (Dan 12:8). The response states that these things are revealed at a later time as these words are concealed, but in the end those who have in-sight (Christians) will understand. The timing is then stated more precisely in Daniel 12:11-12. From the abolishment of the sacri-fice and the abomination of desolation there will be 1290 days. Then after an additional 45 days those who keep waiting will be blessed. Daniel is then told that this is not to be in his lifetime, for he shall die and enter into rest. He shall then rise again at the end of the age and receive his allotted portion (Dan. 12:13).

TIMELINE 5 on the following page shows the timing of the key events recorded in Daniel.

TIMELINE 5 - DANIEL CHAPTER 2, 7, 9, 11 & 12 TIMELINE OF FUTURE THINGS

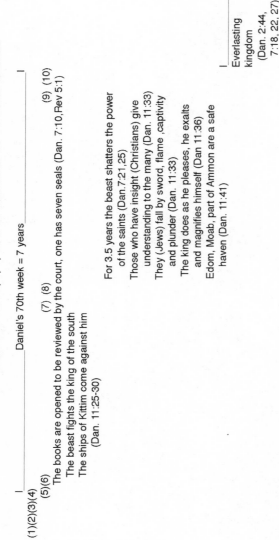

Daniel's 70th week = 7 years

(1)(2)(3)(4)

(5)(6)   (7) (8)   (9) (10)

The books are opened to be reviewed by the court, one has seven seals (Dan. 7:10,Rev 5:1)

The beast fights the king of the south

The ships of Kittim come against him
(Dan. 11:25-30)

For 3.5 years the beast shatters the power
of the saints (Dan.7:21,25)

Those who have insight (Christians) give
understanding to the many (Dan. 11:33)

They (Jews) fall by sword, flame ,captivity
and plunder (Dan. 11:33)

The king does as he pleases, he exalts
and magnifies himself (Dan 11:36)

Edom, Moab, part of Ammon are a safe
haven (Dan. 11:41)

Everlasting
kingdom
(Dan. 2:44,
7:18, 22, 27)

(1) - Ten kings arise out of Rome, some strong, some brittle, Daniel 2:42, 7:24
(2) - Little horn (beast) arises, Daniel 7:8,24
(3) - Beast conquers 3 kings, Dan 7:8
(4) - Firm covenant is signed between the beast and many for 7 years, starts Daniel's 70th week, Daniel 9:27
(5) - Thrones are set up in preparation for judgment court, Daniel 7:9
(6) - Heavenly court sits for judgment, Daniel 7:10,26
(7) - King (beast) becomes enraged at the covenant, Daniel 11:30
(8) - Sacrifice stopped, temple abomination of desolation, Daniel 9:27, 11:31
(9) - Everyone written in the book (of life) is rescued, dead raised, Daniel 12:1,2
(10) - Beast thrown into the lake of fire, Daniel 7:11,9:27, Revelation 19:20

MATTHEW 24

Matthew 24 covers Jesus' key discourse about the end times. It starts with Jesus exiting the temple and the disciples coming up and pointing out the magnificent temple buildings. Jesus surprised them by saying that these buildings will all be totally destroyed and not one stone will be left upon another. After thinking about this, the disciples came to him privately while he sat on the Mount of Olives and asked him three questions (24:3):

1. When will these things happen?
2. What will be the sign of your coming?
3. What will be the sign of the end of the age?

In the context "these things" must be referring to the destruction of the temple. Jesus chose to answer the questions in reverse order.

1	When will these things happen?	24:34
2	What will be the sign of your coming?	24:15-33
3	What will be the sign of the end of the age?	24:4-14

I should point out that this is not a common interpretation. Most ignore the first question assuming it is unanswered or does not relate to the destruction of the temple, creating a big problem in the interpretation of Matthew 24:34. Below, each answer will be addressed in detail.

Question 3: What will be the signs of the end of the age?

The first thing to note is that Christ does not say the end of the age or his coming will be a total surprise. He will send signs in advance. In fact, he lays out the following signs to signal that the end of the age is approaching (Matt. 24:4-14):

Birth pangs, early signs

1. Many false Christs mislead many (Matt 24:5).
2. You will hear of wars and rumors of wars (Matt 24:6).
3. Nation will rise against nation (Matt 24:7).
4. Various famines (Matt 24:7).
5. Various earthquakes (Matt 24:7).

Tribulation signs

6. Christians face tribulation (Matt 24:9).
7. Christians are martyred (Matt 24:9).
8. Christians hated by all nations because of my name (Matt 24:9).
9. Christians fall away, betray and hate one another (Matt 24:10).
10. False prophets arise and mislead many (Matt 24:11).
11. Lawlessness is increased (Matt 24:12).

12. Most people's love grows cold (Matt 24:12).

13. The one who endures will be saved (Matt 24:13).

14. The gospel is preached to the whole world (Matt 24:14).

15. The end (of the age) comes (Matt 24:14).

The birth pangs (Matt 24:5-7) are interesting because the Christian church is constantly watching for them. Within various Christian periodicals you will hear of the increase in earthquakes or the increase in wars. Famines are noted. False Christs are also mentioned. If you think about it, most major religions are built upon a person who claimed to have the answer for what ails man. In this sense they are false Christs. If you look at it that way, then all the birth pangs have occurred or are occurring. They just have not yet given birth to The Tribulation. There is a strong possibility that these birth pangs will be felt in a more dramatic way before the time of The Tribulation.

The Tribulation signs are not yet fulfilled. Although Christians are being martyred, martyrdom has not spread worldwide as implied by Matthew 24:9. It is known from Revelation 13:12-15, that there will be amazing beasts (false prophets) during The Tribulation period that mislead many, which will fulfill sign ten (see list above). The recent increase in lawlessness in the United States and Europe show how quickly sign 11 (see list above) could be fulfilled.

From sign 13 (see list above), one might assume that endurance to the end is a necessary requirement for salvation (24:13). The context here clearly states that there will be worldwide martyrdom of Christians, so enduring until the end is not a requirement for salvation. What this verse tells us is that people who remain loyal to Jesus to the end of their life on earth, however it ends, will be saved (what Christians are saved from will be addressed later). This time period easily lines up with the rescue in Daniel 12:1.

Sign 14 (See list above) is commonly used by various missionaries to say that when the gospel has been taken to every people group then Christ will come back.

"This gospel of the kingdom shall be preached in the
whole world as a testimony to all the nations, and then
the end will come." (Matt. 24:14)

However, the context of this verse is within The Tribulation and Matthew 10:22-23 is a similar passage that implies the work of the evangelist will never be completed. The fulfillment of sign 14 is actually accomplished by God through an angel as revealed in Revelation 14:6-7.

"And I saw another angel flying in midheaven,
having an eternal gospel to preach to those who live
on the earth, and to every nation and tribe and tongue
and people; and he said with a loud voice, "Fear God,
and give Him glory, because the hour of His judgment
has come; worship Him who made the heaven and the
earth and sea and springs of waters." (Rev. 14:6-7)

Question 2; What will be the sign of your coming?

The disciples may not have envisioned Christ's second coming when asking this question. They may have been asking when is your kingdom coming. We know now that his kingdom will not come until he comes again. The disciples asked a question that was not to be completed in their lives but only after Christ was crucified, rose again, and eventually returns to earth.

The answer to this question begins with a severe warning. When those who are in Judea see the abomination of desolation spoken of through Daniel the prophet (Dan. 11:31), they are to flee to the mountains. The warning starts with "therefore" indicating that the persecution discussed in the previous verses is the reason for the urgency of the warning. The warning is extremely urgent as the one on the housetop cannot even take time to go down into his house to gather some things (Matt 24:17-18). The request to "pray that your flight will not be in the winter, or on a Sabbath" (Mt. 24:20) should be prayed now, not after the sign happens. The extra woe to those pregnant and nursing speaks to a time of complete panic in fleeing.

This is also a sign for the start of the great tribulation or the last three and a half years of Daniel's 70th week. The three and a half year period is the same time period that starts in Daniel 11:31 and continues through Daniel 12. It is also the same 3.5 period where the horn (beast) shatters the power of the holy people in Daniel 7. During this time period there will be unequaled distress on the world. Given the events preceding and during WWII , especially for the Jews in the holocaust, this is very foreboding.

Jesus wants to make sure that all Christians are not deceived by false Christs. In Matthew 24:23 Jesus states that his final coming will be with signs so dramatic that they will not be missed. Hence, do not be mislead by great signs that are offered by the false prophets.

Jesus makes it clear that there are Christians on earth during this period of great tribulation. The reference to the elect (Matt 24:22) leaves no doubt.

"Unless those days had been cut short, no life would have been saved; but for the sake of the elect those days will be cut short." (Matt 24:22)

Matthew 24:22 also states that "those days will cut short". The days that are being referenced must be the three and a half years that Daniel 7:21 indicates for the beast to wage war against the saints. These days will be cut short by Christ returning to rapture his elect in Matthew 24:31.

In summary, the signs for Christ's coming according to Matthew 24 are as follows:

- The abomination of desolation (Matt 24:15).
- The worst tribulation in the history of the world (Matt 24:21).
- False Christs and false prophets show great signs (Matt 24:24).
- Heavenly signs (Matt 24:29-30).
  - The sun will be darkened.
  - The moon does not give its light.
  - Stars fall from the sky.
  - Powers of heaven shaken.
  - The sign of the Son of Man appears in the sky.
  - The Son of Man comes on the clouds.

The most important point to note is that when Christ returns he sends forth his angels and they gather his elect from one end of the sky to the other. This is clearly a rapture moment for Christians. Those that remain on the earth are not Christians.

This is the only rapture that Jesus discusses (Mark 13 discusses the same rapture) and therefore, it is logical to assume that this is the rapture. There also is a great parallel passage in Joel 2:29-32 which includes the same heavenly signs. This passage says that everyone who calls on the name of the Lord will be delivered. Many pre-trib believers are actually surprised when they realize their position implies that this is not the rapture but merely Christ's second coming. The reason it cannot be the rapture for those holding a pre-trib position is that it clearly and indisputably comes after the midpoint of The Tribulation. The pre-trib position demands an additional rapture to occur that is never mentioned by Jesus. My position is that if Matthew 24:29-31 reads like a rapture and Jesus does not discuss any other rapture, then logically it is the rapture. The timing of the rapture in this passage is easily placed at the same time as the rescue of everyone written in the book and the resurrection of those asleep in Daniel 12:1.

Question 1: When will these things happen?

The disciples first question was, "When will the Temple be destroyed?" (Matt 24:3). Did Christ answer this question or not? As I noted above, my position is that Jesus answered the three questions in reverse order. The answer to "When will these things happen?" is given in verse 34.

"Truly I say to you, this generation will not pass away
until all these things take place." (Matt 24:34)

The temple was destroyed in 70 AD, which was before the people of Christ's generation passed away. This position addresses a controversial verse and allows Christ to have provided a complete answer to the three questions in 24:3 in reverse order.

Accepting that Matthew 24:34 is the answer to the first question is preferable over the two other choices I have heard:

    a)   A claim that all the preceding happened within a generation of Christ (Preterist position).

    b)   A claim that "this generation" (Matt 24:34) is really a reference to the church age.

A Concluding Thought

A common argument for the pre-trib rapture is that no other position allows for the imminent (i.e., could happen at any time) return of Christ. In other words, if all the signs stated by Christ in Matthew 24 had to come true before the rapture, then it could not be imminent. Therefore, the events in Matthew 24:31 are not the rapture but his second coming.

> "And He will send forth His angels with a great trumpet and they will gather together His elect from the four winds, from one end of the sky to the other."
> (Matt 24:31)

Scripture never states the return of Christ is imminent. One passage commonly used to prove an imminent return position is Matthew 24:36-39 where it states that no one knows the day or the hour of Christ's return. However, this verse doesn't support the imminent return of Christ. In context, the passage is clearly talking about Jesus' coming in Matthew 24:30 and it is accompanied with signs as indicated in Matt 24:32-33. The fact that no one knows the day or the hour does not mean it is without signs; the point is that the exact day is unknown. Jesus again illustrates in Matthew 25 that the exact time of his coming is unknown.

Jesus gives a parable of ten virgins who were waiting for the bridegroom to return. The virgins knew the bridegroom would return soon, but they did not know exactly when.

For those who hold to the imminent return of Christ, they must consider the fact that Christ's return could not always have been imminent. The return of Christ could not be imminent for the first century church when the Scripture was written due to the following required events prior to the start of The Tribulation.

- The destruction of Jerusalem (Daniel 9)
- The fall of Rome (Daniel 2)
- People going back and forth and knowledge increased (Daniel 12)
- The rise of ten kings (Daniel 7)
- The rise of another king (Daniel 7)
- Worldwide population to support a 200,000,000 man army from the east (Revelation 9)
- Technology for all to see the dead two witnesses (Revelation 11)

The above list was clearly not fulfilled when most of the New Testament was written in 40-70 AD. Therefore, it is logical to conclude that the imminent return of Christ can not be the interpretation of what the Bible says, because then the Bible would not have been accurate when it was written.

TIMELINE 6 depicts the events of Matthew.

TIMELINE 6 - MATTHEW 24 TIMELINE

Daniel's 70th week = 7 years

(1)(2)   (3)   (4)
                                                                   (5) (6) (7)

False Messiahs (vs 5)
Wars, rumors of wars (vs 6)
Nation will rise against nation (vs 7)
Kingdom against kingdom (vs 7)
Famines and earthquakes (vs 7)

Christians handed over to be persecuted and
    put to death (vs 9)
Christians hated by all nations because of Christ (vs 9)
Many turn away from faith, betray one another (vs 10)
False prophets appear and deceive many (vs 11)
Wickedness increases, love grows cold (vs 12)

The great unequaled distress on the world (vs 21)
False prophets perform great signs (vs 24)

(1) - Temple abomination of desolation Daniel 9:27, 11:31, Matthew 24:15
(2) - Those in Judea must flee to the mountains, Matthew 24:16
(3) - Gospel of the kingdom is preached to the whole world, Matthew 24:14
(4) - The end of the age, Matthew 24:14
(5) - The sun will be darkened, moon will not give its light, stars fall from the sky, heavenly bodies will be shaken, Matthew 24:29
(6) - The sign of the Son of Man appears in heaven, every one mourns, Matthew 24:30
(7) - The Son of man comes with great power and glory and his angels gather (rapture) his elect, Matthew 24:30,31

THESSALONIANS

There are three passages in Thessalonians that contribute to our understanding of the end times. The first passage is the best overall description of the rapture provided by Paul.

1 Thessalonians 4:13-18

Let's list the facts given by Paul in this passage.

- We should not grieve over those who are asleep (dead).
- God will bring with Him those who have fallen asleep in Jesus.
- The Lord will descend with a shout, with the voice of the archangel and the trumpet of God.
- The Dead in Christ will rise first.
- We who remain will be caught up together with them.
- We shall always be with the Lord.

Paul has a similar passage in 1 Corinthians 15:51-52. This passage adds that we will be changed in a twinkling of an eye; we will take on an imperishable body. These passages are accepted as being rapture descriptions by pre-trib, mid-trib, pre-wrath, and post-trib believers. The reason for their universal acceptance is that there is no timing associated with them. When looking at potential rapture descriptions elsewhere in the Bible, they need to be reviewed for consistency with 1 Thessalonians 4:13-18. The passage in Daniel 12:1-2 is very consistent in that it mentions both the resurrection from the dead of believers as well as the rescue of living believers. Matthew 24:29-31 is focusing on the signs before Christ's return and fails to mention the raising from the dead of believers. That being said, there is no inconsistency.

2 Thessalonians 1:6-8

The second brief passage that I find interesting is:

"For after all it is only just for God to repay with affliction those who afflict you, and to give relief to you who are afflicted and to us as well when the Lord Jesus will be revealed from heaven with His mighty angels in flaming fire, dealing out retribution to those who do not know God and to those who do not obey the gospel of our Lord Jesus." (2 Thess 1:6-8)

This passage indicates that we, as Christians, will get relief from our afflictions when Christ returns to hand out retribution to our enemies. This is described as a single streaming event in which we get relief, while those who afflict us get retribution. This passage presents a problem to pre-trib believers because it describes Christ as handing out retribution immediately following the relief given to believers including potentially Paul himself.

To support a pre-trib rapture position, there would need to be a nearly seven year gap to allow for the beast to be in control.

The verse also indicates that he is coming with his mighty angels in flaming fire. In the gospel of Luke, Jesus states,

> "I have come to cast fire upon the earth; and how I wish it were already kindled!" (Luke 12:49)

Both of these texts mention Christ's coming with fire and are therefore totally consistent with the events at the beginning of Revelation 8.

> "Then the angel took the censer and filled it with the fire of the altar, and threw it to the earth; and there followed peals of thunder and sounds and flashes of lightning and an earthquake." (Rev 8:5)

> "The first sounded, and there came hail and fire, mixed with blood, and they were thrown to the earth; and a third of the earth was burned up, and a third of the trees were burned up, and all the green grass was burned up. The second angel sounded, and something like a great mountain burning with fire was thrown into the sea; and a third of the sea became blood, and a third of the creatures which were in the sea and had life, died; and a third of the ships were destroyed." (Rev 8:7-9)

Therefore, it is logical to assume that 2 Thessalonians 1:6-8 positions the coming of Christ with the events of Revelation 8.

2 Thessalonians 2:1-12

The third passage to look at is 2 Thessalonians 2:1-12. This passage is in response to the Thessalonians being worried that they may have missed the coming of our Lord Jesus and our gathering to him (the rapture). Remember that Paul gave no timing information as to the rapture in 1 Thessalonians 4:13-18. He is going to correct that in this passage.

> "Now we request you, brethren, with regard to the coming of our Lord Jesus Christ and our gathering together to him, that you not be quickly shaken from your composure or be disturbed either by a spirit or a message or a letter as if from us to the effect that the day of the Lord has come. Let no one in any way deceive you, for it will not come unless the apostasy comes first, and the man of lawlessness is revealed, the son of destruction, who opposes and exalts himself above every so-called god or object of worship, so that he takes his seat in the temple of God, displaying himself as being God."(2 Thessalonians 2:1-4)

The simple interpretation of this passage is that Paul says the Thessalonians should not be shaken from their composure by a false message or letter. Paul says "let no one in any way deceive you!" Our gathering to Christ will not come unless the apostasy comes first. Prior to Christ's return, the man of lawlessness (the beast) will be revealed and he will oppose and exalt himself above all gods (Dan 11:31, 36). He will take his seat in the temple displaying himself as being God. Paul knows that this event will be so big and disruptive that they will know of it. Not only that, since news travels slowly, Paul is stating that even after that event, they will have time to hear of it before the rapture. The beast will be in the temple (abomination of desolation) before the rapture. This warning "to not be deceived" is entirely consistent with what Jesus stated in Matthew 24. Some that hold to the pre-trib rapture position work around this straightforward interpretation by saying Paul is stating that before the final judgment comes, the beast takes his place in the temple. This sequence, if not related to the rapture, would not give the Thessalonians any comfort and would be meaningless for Paul to say in response to the Thessalonians' concern that they had missed the rapture. Note in verse 3 Paul commands the Thessalonians to not be deceived referring to these events. If they were raptured 3.5 years earlier, in a pre-trib rapture, there is no chance they would be deceived about these tribulation events.

The pre-trib position often interprets 2 Thessalonians 2:6 by saying that Paul is stating the church is restraining the beast now through the in-dwelling Holy Spirit, and once the church is removed the Holy Spirit will no longer restrain. Therefore, the church must be removed before the beast is unconstrained. This pre-trib position is compromised by the existence of believers during The Tribulation period, which are presumably led to Christ through the Holy Spirit and have the Holy Spirit dwelling within them. The likely restrainer, in my opinion, is God through his angels, most likely Michael (see Rev 12:7-9). Viewing the church as the restrainer would turn this verse into a support for the pre-trib rapture, but in my opinion there is little evidence that supports the position of the church as the restrainer.

REVELATION 1, 2 AND 3

Since most of our discussion will be focused on Revelation 4 – 22, I will offer only a brief discussion of the first three chapters.

Revelation 1

This introduction is important as it indicates the timing of future events is soon; the time is near (Rev 1:1-3). The near return of Christ is a little bit of a quandary as it has been nearly 2000 years since his death. The Preterist position solves this quandary by saying that these events occurred in 70 AD. If everything actually happened that is supposed to happen when Christ returns then it would be an excellent solution. However, it is clear that not all the events referred to in Revelation have happened. Reviewing the trumpet judgments it is clear that they did not. The Pre-trib position says that the verses imply that his return is imminent (could happen at any time). Revelation 1:1-3 does not say that "the things which must soon take place" are imminent, but that they are coming soon; the time is near. Two thousand years later, the meaning of the passage and the use of the words soon and near remain a mystery. My position is that it is an individual warning that needs to be heeded individually. By that I mean it is less than 120 years away for all of us; for after each of us die, our souls go to heaven but our bodies sleep. We are awakened when Christ returns. God clearly wants us to know there is very little time for us before these events occur.

The other thing to note from Revelation 1 is the glorious state of the Lord and Savior (verses 12-16). He is no longer the Lord in a humbled, sacrificed body. He, in all His power, is the one dictating the letters to the seven churches that follow in chapters two and three. The Christ in Revelation 1 is the Christ that Christians pray to today.

Revelation 2 and 3

The second and third chapters of Revelation contain seven letters to seven churches. Each of the seven letters have the same general structure.

1. Description of Christ as author.
2. The general state of the church.
3. Commands from the Lord Jesus Christ.
4. A reward described for those who overcome (the faithful).

It should be noted that Christ is addressing actual churches. Similar to today, some of the churches are more faithful to Christ than others. Some of the content of these letters may contain verses with prophetic fulfillment. The one verse used to support the Pre-trib rapture position from these letters is Revelation 3:10 in the passage to the church of Philadelphia.

"Because you have kept the word of My perseverance, I also will keep you from the hour of testing, that hour which is about to come upon the whole world, to test those who dwell on the earth." Rev 3:10

Revelation 3:10 does seem to be prophetic as do some of the other texts in the seven letters.

To use this verse to support the pre-trib position, three assumptions must be made.

(1) The hour of testing must be the seven years of Daniel's 70th week

(2) The phrase "keep you from" must refer to the rapture.

(3) The church in Philadelphia must represent the whole church of the end times just prior to Daniel's 70th week.

There is no biblical support to make these assumptions. That is to say, there is no Scripture that states the church at Philadelphia represents the entire church, just prior to the rapture. The phrase "keep you from" does not demand removal from the earth. There is no Scripture that states the hour of testing is equivalent to the seven year tribulation. There are various "hours" discussed during The Tribulation. The hour of God's judgment in Revelation 14:7 is one such reference. Thus, Revelation 3:10 does not strongly support any rapture timing position.

REVELATION 4, 5 AND 6

Many times, in the past studies of the end-times, I just glossed over Revelation 4 & 5 so I could get to the seals being broken in chapter six. I never really noticed when the seals were first discussed, and I lost sight of the fact that these seals were keeping a book (scroll) closed. I have come to believe that Revelation 4 & 5 lay crucial groundwork for the understanding of Revelation 6 and Revelation 7.

Revelation 4 and 5

There are many symbols in these chapters, such as beasts with eyes covering them (which is likely symbolic of an all-knowing God). Instead of fully understanding each symbol this study will focus on how these chapters fill in and expand a key part of the timeline given in Daniel 7.

In Revelation 4, when John arrives in heaven, God is sitting on the center throne. There are 24 other thrones set up and the 24 elders are sitting on them. The elders then proceed to fall down before God and worship Him. Revelation 4 and 5 can be placed in the Daniel 7 sequence as follows:

Kingdom 1 - Babylon, lion with wings of an eagle

Kingdom 2 - Media Persia, bear

Kingdom 3 - Greece, leopard

Kingdom 4 - Rome, dreadful and terrifying
　　　　　　Descends into ten kingdoms, ten horns

Final Kingdom - Beast, Little horn
　　　　　　Utters great boasts
　　　　　　Thrones in heaven set up for
　　　　　　judgment
　　　　　　God takes his seat
　　　　　　Revelation 4 and 5
　　　　　　Books are opened
　　　　　　Beast continues to boast in power
　　　　　　Beast slain, given to burning fire

Jesus, the Son of Man, is given an eternal kingdom over all

It is clear from the beginning of Revelation 5 that the books mentioned in Daniel 7:10 are not yet opened. In fact, John is very concerned (5:4), to the point of weeping, that a certain book cannot be opened because of the seven seals that are holding it closed.

"I saw in the right hand of Him who sat on the throne
a book written inside and on the back, sealed up with
seven seals." (Rev 5:1)

The books were not discussed in Daniel 7, but it can be assumed they contained information needed for the court. The books needed for the court are mentioned in Revelation 20:12:

"And I saw the dead, the great and the small,
standing before the throne, and books were opened;
and another book was opened, which is the book
of life; and the dead were judged from the things,
which were written in the books, according to their
deeds."(Rev 20:12)

The two books mentioned are the book of life and the books of deeds. These are the obvious books for judgment. The books that recorded everyone's deeds contain records of everything everyone has done both good and bad. Most people are not proud of their record of sins including every selfish act and every time they did not put God first in their life. Based on this book no one will be allowed into heaven. Fortunately, God in His ultimate mercy created another path to heaven, and everyone, whose name is written in the book of life, will be allowed to enter heaven. The book of life is mentioned many times in the Bible.

- Psalm 69:28 - the book of life records the names of the righteous

- Daniel 12:1 - Everyone found written in the book will be rescued

- Philippians 4:3 - Paul's fellow workers are in the book of life

- Revelation 3:5 - Those who overcome will not be erased from the book of life

- Revelation 13:8 - Everyone not written in the book of life will worship the beast, this passage, being after Revelation 5, is the first to state that it is the Lamb's book of life.

- Revelation 17:8 - Those not written in the book of life will show great wonder after the beast at his appearance.

- Revelation 20:15 - Those not written in the book of life will be thrown into the lake of fire.

- Revelation 21:27 - Only those written in the Lamb's book of life will be allowed in heaven.

In Revelation 5:4 it states that John wept and wept because no one was able to open a particular book. This sorrow can only be felt for the book of life, clearly not the book of our deeds. As an added note, in Daniel 12:4, Daniel is told to conceal and seal up the book until the end of time. The context would lead one to believe the reference is to the book of life mentioned in Daniel 12:1. In Revelation 5:5, one of the elders tells John that the Lion from the tribe of Judah has overcome so he can open the book. The Lion of the tribe of Judah then appears as a Lamb and takes the book from the right hand of God and the 24 elders and the angels fall down and worship the Lamb who is able to break the seals. Jesus could not open the book of life unless he overcame and sacrificed his life for those written in the book. It is noteworthy that there is no mention of the church in heaven at this time. This is entirely logical because the court cannot reach its verdict on each individual until the book of life is opened. After the seals are opened on the book in Revelation 6 -8 there is no more mention of the book. This dramatic book with its dramatic opening is a mystery and has no purpose unless it is understood to be the Lamb's book of life. The most logical conclusion to all of this is that the seals are sealing up the book of life that Daniel was told to seal up in Daniel 12:4. This book of life will be opened once the seals are removed. The logical point for the rapture is when the book of life is opened.

The Pre-trib rapture position would prefer the church to be in heaven at this time and they put forward two arguments to support their position.

1. The first is that John's going up to heaven in the spirit (Rev 4:1-2) represents the rapture of the church.
2. The second argument is that 12 of the 24 elders represent the church.

It has always been difficult for me to accept either one of these arguments as they appear to be mere speculation. Assuming the sealed book is the Lamb's book of life, then it is logical that the church is not in heaven prior to its opening.

Revelation 4-5 give us a crucial picture. The one breaking the seals in Chapter 6 is Christ breaking the seals on the book of life, preparing to judge the world.

Revelation 6

The Lamb now proceeds to open the seals of the book of life. The seals present in a logical, chronological order what is to take place during the end times. From the sequence in Daniel 7, the beast is in power uttering great boasts before the books are opened. This is the only timing information in the Bible as to when the breaking of the seals takes place.

Seal 1 - Revelation 6:1-2

The first seal is a white horse. The rider (likely the beast) is given a crown and he goes out conquering. The white color of the horse symbolizes something that will appear good to those that dwell upon the earth. The crown, given to the rider, likely symbolizes that he is put in power by the people, possibly in an election.

Seal 2 - Revelation 6:3-4

The second horse is red symbolizing the blood of worldwide war. The rider (the beast) has a great sword symbolizing great power.

Seal 3 - Revelation 6:5-6

The third horse clearly symbolizes famine, likely caused in part by the wars of the second seal.

Seal 4 - Revelation 6:7-8

The fourth horse was pale or ashen. The rider of the horse was death and he was sent to kill, impacting one fourth of the earth with famine, disease, and wild beasts of the earth.

Seal 5 - Revelation 6:9-11

This seal represents Christian martyrs and their souls pleading before God to judge those that dwell upon the earth and to avenge their blood. They are given white robes but told that more of their brethren are to be killed. This clearly aligns with Daniel 7:21, 25, where the beast wears down the saints of the Highest One (Christ).

Seal 6 - Revelation 6:12-17

This seal marks the beginning of the end for the beast. The following signs appear:

- A great earthquake.
- The sun becomes black.
- The moon becomes red.
- Stars of the sky fall to the earth.

- The sky is split apart like a scroll.
- Every mountain and island is moved.

Upon witnessing these events those on the earth hide in caves and rocks from God and the coming wrath of the Lamb. The people on earth now tremble and say " the great day of their wrath has come and who is able to stand?" (Rev 6:17) This pronouncement implies that the wrath of the Lamb has not yet begun. Clearly God's wrath is started just prior to the blowing of the first trumpet in Revelation 8.

The similarity between seal 6 and the signs of Christ's coming in Matthew 24 jump off the page. In Matthew 24:29-30 it states:

- The sun will be darkened.
- The moon does not give its light.
- Stars fall from the sky.
- Powers of heaven shaken.
- The sign of the Son of Man appears in the sky.

It is also important to note that the first six seals are represented in Matthew 24, not just seal 6.

Revelation	Matthew
Seal 1, war	24:6
Seal 2, war	24:6
Seal 3, famine	24:7
Seal 4, famine, disease, wild beasts	24:7

Seal 5, Christians martyred	24:9
Seal 6, Signs of Christ's return	24:29-30

Although the first six seals are included in Matthew 24, it is clear that none of the trumpet judgments are. The first trumpet involves fire destroying one third of the earth as described in Revelation 8:7. That is a sign that Christ would certainly mention if it were before his return in Matthew 24:30. The evidence is conclusive, the point in time of Matthew 24:29-30 is the same point in time as Seal 6. The logical deduction is that Christ returns to gather up his elect sometime after Seal 6 is broken and before trumpet 1 is sounded. Since God's wrath is announced in 6:17 and definitely started just prior to the blowing of the first trumpet in Revelation 8, the position, that Matthew 24:29-31 is the rapture, is consistent with the pre-wrath position so there is no conflict with 1 Thessalonians 1:10 or 5:9. There is confirming evidence in chapter 7 for this position.

TIMELINE 7 shows Matthew 24 and the events of Revelation through chapter 6.

TIMELINE 7 - REVELATION 4, 5, & 6 WITH THE MATTHEW 24 TIMELINE

Daniel's 70th week = 7 years

(1)(2)   (3)   (4)
                 (5) (6) (7)

(8)   (S1)   (S2)   (S3)   (S4)   (S5)   (S6)

False Messiahs (Mt.24:5)
Wars, rumors of wars (Mt.24:6)
Nation will rise against nation (Mt.24:7)
Kingdom against kingdom (Mt.24:7)
Famines and earthquakes (Mt.24:7)

Christians handed over to be persecuted and
put to death (Mt.24:9)
Christians hated by all nations due to Christ (Mt.24:9)
Many turn away from faith, betray one another (Mt.24:9)
False prophets appear and deceive many (Mt.24:10)
Wickedness increases, love grows cold (Mt.24:12)

The great unequaled distress on the world (Mt.24:21)
False prophets perform great signs (Mt.24:24)

(1) - Temple abomination of desolation Daniel 9:27, 11:31, Matthew 24:15
(2) - Those in Judea must flee to the mountains, Matthew 24:16
(3) - Gospel of the kingdom is preached to the whole world, Matthew 24:14
(4) - The end of the age, Matthew 24:14
(5) - The sun will be darkened, moon will not give its light, stars fall from the sky heavenly bodies will be shaken, Matthew 24:29
(6) - The sign of the Son of Man appears in heaven, every one mourns, Matthew 24:30
(7) - The Son of man comes with great power and glory and his angels gather (rapture) his elect, Matthew 24:30,31
(8) - God is seated on his throne in heaven, and the 24 elders are on their thrones, Revelation 4:2-4
(S1) - (S6) - The first six seals on the book of life are broken by Christ, Revelation 6

REVELATION 7

The scene at the end of Revelation 6 depicts a world wanting to hide from the Lamb and the great day of his wrath. The timing of the end of Revelation 6 is the same as Matthew 24:29-30. Christ is just about to return and gather his elect from the four corners of the earth. Revelation 7 provides added information about that time period.

Revelation 7 opens with four angels being granted authority to harm the earth and the sea. However, they may not harm the earth, sea, or trees until the bond-servants of the living God have been sealed on their foreheads. The number sealed was 144,000, that is, 12,000 from each of the 12 tribes of Israel. The precise wording leads me to think that the number and the origin of the people should be taken literally. As to how the sealing works, or what it looks like, we are left to wonder. The 144,000 were clearly being sealed because they were going to go through the next events on earth (the trumpets). Revelation 7 proves that Israel is still central to God's future plans. An obvious question might be, "Where did the rest of the Christian brethren go, was this all that was left after the persecution of the beast?" The answer is provided in the following verses and in Matthew 24:31. The rest of the brethren were raptured from the four corners of the earth as stated in Matthew 24:31 and mentioned in Daniel 12:1.

The results of this gathering are seen in heaven. There is now a great multitude, clothed in white robes, which no one could count (Rev 7:9-17). This multitude must be the raptured saints from every nation, tribe, peoples and tongues. Those that have been raptured are crying out in worship of God and the Lamb. In this scene, the 24 elders are still there and all the angels are there worshipping as well. What a glorious moment!

Then John is asked by an elder about the identity of the people in the white robes. He does not give the answer but rather one of the elders answers.

> "Then one of the elders answered, saying to me,
> "These in white robes, who are they, and where did
> they come from?" I said to him, "My Lord, you know."
> And he said to me, "These are the ones who have
> come out of the great tribulation and they
> have washed their robes and made them white in the
> blood of the lamb."" (Rev 7:13-14)

They serve God day and night and are no longer faced with hunger, thirst, or intense heat. The Lamb is their Shepherd; He guides them to living water and God wipes every tear from their eyes (Rev 7:15-17). It is clear from this passage that although these brethren went through the great tribulation, they are being cared for and eternally comforted by Christ and with out a doubt, they are loved by God. For those who persevered through The Tribulation, it was well worth the effort.

In Matthew 24 and Revelation 7 there is clear evidence that there is a world- wide rapture during The Tribulation and it occurs well past the midpoint; that is, after the reference in Matthew 24:15 to the Abomination of Desolation spoken of by Daniel the prophet in Daniel 11:31. This rapture is also after the events of the six seals including the martyrdom of Christians spoken of in Seal 5 and in Daniel 7:21,25.

For many years I believed that the rapture was after the sixth seal just as the sequence appears in Revelation 6, 7, and 8. Recently, I became convinced that the book (scroll) that the seals are on is the Lamb's book of life. If that is the case and the events of the first six seals were necessary in the symbolic opening of the book of life, then the rapture would not occur until after the 7th seal is broken allowing the book (scroll) to be opened. As part of the judgment process the books are opened as stated in Daniel 7:10. The book of life with the names of everyone who is saved is one of those books as stated in Revelation 20:12, 21:27.

It is interesting to note in the opening of the first six seals the Greek word used for "when" (Rev. 6:1, 3, 5, 7,9,12) is *hote* and for the seventh seal the Greek word for "when" (Rev. 8:1) is *hotan*.

"Then I saw when (hote) the Lamb broke one of the seven seals, and I heard one of the four living creatures saying as with a voice of thunder, "Come.""
(Rev 6:1)

"When (hotan) the Lamb broke the seventh seal, there was silence in heaven for about half an hour." (Rev 8:1).

The definitions of the words hote and hotan are very similar yet slightly different according to the Analytical Greek Lexicon;

Hote – when, at the time that, at what time

Hotan – when, whenever, in case of, on occasion

The context of hotan in Revelation 8:1 and the fact that a different word is given by the Holy Spirit, through John, gives reason to believe that there is something different about the "when" of the seventh seal. Also, the wording for the sixth seal implies that John was seeing it opened in his vision, whereas the wording for the seventh seal does not demand that he saw it opened. It is possible that Revelation 8:1 is referring to a past event.

A logical sequence of events could be:

- The sixth seal is opened (Rev 6:12).

- The 144,000 are sealed for their protection (Rev 7:4).

- The seventh seal is opened (referred to in Rev 8:1).

- Immediately the book of life can be opened to symbolically allow judgment.

- The dead in Christ rise first (1 Thess 4:16).

- The Christians who are not of the 144,000 are raptured (Matt 24:31, 1 Thess 4:17, Rev 7:13-14).

- There is silence in heaven for half an hour (Rev 8:1).

REVELATION 8, 9 AND 10

Revelation 8

As noted previously, chapter 8 opens with silence in heaven for about half an hour immediately following the opening of the seventh seal, enabling the opening of the book of life. This is a solemn occasion because Christ is about to bring his prophesied fiery judgment to earth.

> "I have come to cast fire upon the earth; and how I wish it were already kindled!" (Luke 12:49)

The seventh seal brings forth the seven trumpets. Hence, we know all trumpet events occur after the seventh seal. The seventh seal itself also brings fire down from a heavenly alter along with thunder, lightning, and an earthquake. The trumpet judgments are extremely severe.

Trumpet 1	Hail and fire hurled to earth, $1/3$ of the earth burns (Rev 8:7).
Trumpet 2	Huge mountain of fire into sea, $1/3$ of the sea to blood (Rev 8:8).

Trumpet 3	Great fiery star falls on the rivers, $\frac{1}{3}$ of rivers turn bitter and many die from it (Rev 8:10).
Trumpet 4	A third of the stars, moon and sun grow dark, and a third of the day and night have no light (Rev 8:12).
Trumpet 5	Woe 1 - Supernatural locusts torment mankind for 5 months, they long to die but do not (Rev 9:1-11)
Trumpet 6	Woe 2 - 200 million horsemen come from beyond the Euphrates river and $\frac{1}{3}$ of mankind is killed (Rev 9:13-19)
Trumpet 7	Woe 3 – The kingdom of the world given over to the Lord and Christ and He shall reign forever, lightening, thunder, an earthquake and a terrible hailstorm (Rev 11:15).

The final three trumpets are to be even more severe. They are introduced by the angel with the words "Woe, Woe, Woe."

Then I looked, and I heard an eagle flying in mid-heaven, saying with a loud voice, "Woe, woe, woe to those who dwell on the earth, because of the remaining blasts of the trumpet of the three angels who are about to sound!" (Rev. 8:13)

None of the events in Revelation 8 were included in Matthew 24 as signs for Christ's return. Each event is so dramatic and cataclysmic that it is unlikely that Jesus would leave them out. The strong conclusion is that the rapture of Matthew 24:31 occurred prior to the sounding of the first trumpet.

The Preterist position holds that nearly all of Revelation has been fulfilled by 70 AD. While many of the seal events such as war and famine did occur in the first century, it is clear that the trumpet events did not occur by 70AD, which makes the Preterist position untenable.

Revelation 9

Chapter 9 begins with Trumpet 5, which is the first woe. The description of this woe takes 11 verses and is filled with symbolic imagery. The text states that a star falls from heaven and he has given to him the key to open a shaft into the abyss. Out of this shaft, smoke comes forth and darkens the sky, and out of the smoke comes locusts that have the sting of a scorpion. This sting would torment man for 5 months but would not kill him. Revelation 9:4 states that the 144,000 that were sealed in Revelation 7:4 are not stung. This statement also confirms the fact that the 144,000 remained on earth.

It is clear that these are not ordinary locusts but demonic powers. Some commentators have tried to link the locusts with man-made tanks and helicopters, but the locust's supernatural appearance and the fact that they are commanded by the demon that is over the abyss (Rev 9:1, 11) seems to indicate otherwise. One key thing to note is that the stings last for 5 months implying that The Great Tribulation has yet some length of time to run.

The angel who blows the sixth trumpet is told to release four angels who are bound at the river Euphrates. These angels will enable the killing of one third of mankind. The loss of life will be in battle with an army of 200 million horsemen from East of the Euphrates. The people are killed by fire, smoke and brimstone, created by these horsemen. The description to me implies that the horsemen are human and not angelic but that can be argued either way. If they are human, then this event could not happen until there were 200 million available soldiers East of the Euphrates. There were not even 1 billion people on earth until the eighteenth century. Around 1995 China claimed that they could raise a 200 million man army. Once again, the description of these horsemen may be symbolic or perhaps it's just the best way John had to describe what he saw. Clearly these are not normal horses because Revelation 9:19 states that their power is in their mouths and their tails.

After mankind encounters the severe devastation of the fifth and sixth trumpets, the remnant of mankind does not repent or turn to God (Rev 9:20-21). Rather, they continue to:

- worship demons and idols
- murder
- practice sorceries, immorality, and thefts

Revelation 9 ends without the sounding of the trumpet by the seventh angel. This event is not described until chapter 11 and can be used as a way to place the events of chapter 11 on our time line.

Revelation 10

Revelation 10 is a difficult chapter because God has intentionally left it a mystery.

An extremely large and powerful angel appears. He has a little, open book in his hand. This could be the book of life because it would be open at this point, and the person holding it has Christ-like features. It may not be the book of life because a different word is used for this book, which indicates its small-ness., However, it may just appear small in relationship to the one holding it. John is later told to eat the book, which makes little sense for the book of life. Note that the angel has many things about him that are Christ-like.

- He has one foot on the land and one foot on the sea, indicating that he has authority over both land and sea.

- His face is like the sun and his feet are like pillars of fire. This matches up well with the description of the resurrected Christ given in Revelation 1:15-16.

- The angel cries out like the roar of a lion, and when he does, seven peals of thunder sound. John starts to record what is said, but he hears a voice from heaven telling him to seal up what is said. Christ is referred to as a lion in Revelation 5:5.

Although Christ appears in the old testament many times referred to as an angel, which literally means messenger, John would likely recognize Christ and call him by name or the reference "son of man" as he did in Revelation 1. The meaning of the peals of thunder is intended to be sealed up until the end, so one should not speculate on the peals of thunder. The angel then swears an oath by the Creator of all things (not Christ like) that when the seventh angel sounds then the mystery of God is finished. Then the voice, which told John to seal up the words of the peals of thunder, tells John to take the book, which is opened in the hand of the angel, and eat it. This book will make his stomach bitter but in his mouth it will be as sweet as honey. Perhaps the meaning is that God's word is always sweet to the taste even when it speaks of judgment.

If I sound uncertain about the events in this chapter then I have successfully portrayed my position. If pressed for a position I would say;

The angel is likely not Christ.

The book is likely not the book of life.

I have no clue about the 7 peals of thunder.

I do not know why the book is sweet in the mouth but bitter in the stomach.

After eating the book, the first sequential prophecy (Revelation 4 – Revelation 10) given to John is completed. John is then told, ""You must prophesy again concerning many peoples and nations and tongues and kings" (Rev 10:11). **This statement is the key one for understanding the chronology of Revelation.**

Everything in chapter 4 through chapter 10 was in chronological order. This was emphasized by the sequence of seals and trumpets. What follows after chapter 10 is *not* continuing in the same chronological order. Revelation 11 through 22 records three more prophetic chronologies which overlay on the chronological time- line created from Revelation 4 through 10. The three prophecies to follow can be broken down as follows:

- Many people (a perspective from the temple) Revelation 11

- Nations and tongues - Revelation 12-16

- Kings and conclusion- Revelation 17-22.

REVELATION 11

Revelation 11 starts the next prophecy given to John. The timing of the events in this chapter do not immediately follow the events in chapter 10. This is fulfilling Revelation 10:11, where John is told, "You must prophesy again concerning many peoples and nations and tongues and kings". This prophecy describes a time period that overlaps the time period of Revelation 4-10 and will be located on our timeline by text at the end of Revelation 11.

At the beginning of Revelation 11, John is given a measuring rod and is told to get up and measure the temple of God and those that worship in it. He's told to leave out the court, which is outside, because it has been given over to the nations. Scripture indicates that this is a real temple on earth during The Tribulation period. This temple is required for sacrifices to be offered according to the Jewish law given to Moses.

John is then told that the nations will control the holy city with troops for 42 months or 3.5 years. During this time, the temple will be miraculously protected by two witnesses. These witnesses cannot be harmed for 1260 days, which equals the 42 months that the nations will control the city. The start of these 42 months coincides with the sacrifice being stopped in Daniel 9:27, and in Daniel 11:31 and Matthew 24:15. This is the point in time that the abomination of desolation is set up, and the nation of Israel must flee to the mountains. God miraculously protects the temple during this time. Those who attack these two witnesses are killed by fire flowing out of their mouths. How this works, clearly with the supernatural power of God overcoming the age of modern weaponry, is movie worthy. In 11:6 it says that these witnesses have great power.

> "These have the power to shut up the sky so that rain will not fall during the days of their prophesying, and they have power over the waters to turn them into blood as well as to strike the earth with every plague as often as they desire." (Rev 11:6. See also Rev 8:8; 9:18)

Some of the power that the two witnesses have can be lined up with the trumpet events. When the two witnesses finish their testimony they will be killed by the beast. Their bodies are not buried. Rather, they are left in the streets for the world to see. The fact that for three and a half days the world will be able to look at their bodies is easily fulfilled in the age of web cams. The earliest in history, that this world- wide viewing could have taken place, would be during the age of live satellite television, a technology that was not available until 1965. Thus, the Tribulation was not imminent and therefore Christ's return was not imminent until technology was available to fulfill this prophecy. I believe that when this prophecy was given to John, God's time table for the internet was already in place and certainly not a surprise to him.

The death of these two witnesses is cause for great celebration on earth. All of the disastrous events on earth are blamed upon them. They lay on the streets dead for three and a half days and then are brought back to life while the whole world watches.

The world is now terrified as God calls them up to heaven. There is a great earthquake that destroys a tenth of the city and 7,000 people are killed. Revelation 11:14 ties this point in time to the end of the second woe (the sixth trumpet). The third woe (the seventh trumpet) is coming quickly. Some believe the three and a half year period, of the two witnesses, occurs in the first half of The Tribulation, but this time marker of ending after the second woe (sixth trumpet), but before the third woe (seventh trumpet), clearly puts these events in the last three and a half years.

The sounding of the seventh trumpet in Revelation 11:15 announces that the everlasting reign of Christ over the world has begun. Daniel 7:13-14 also clearly states that the Son of Man (Christ) would reign. At the start of Christ's reign, the Christians are given dominion over the earth and will actually reign with Christ (Dan 7:18, 27)! The seventh trumpet marks the end of Daniel's seventieth week. The great tribulation and the mystery of God are finished;

> "But in the days of the voice of the seventh angel,
> when he is about to sound, then the mystery of
> God is finished, as He preached to His servants the
> prophets." (Rev 10:7)

TIMELINE 8 looks at the last 3.5 years of The Tribulation with the events through Revelation 11.

TIMELINE 8 - REVELATION 6-11 WITH THE LAST 3.5 YEARS OF MATTHEW 24 TIMELINE

Last 3.5 years of Daniel's 70th week

(1)(2)   (3)   (4)
                                              (5)(6)(7)

(8)(T1)-(T6)
                                                        (9)(T7)

Christians handed over to be persecuted and be put to death (Matt. 24:9)
Christians hated by all nations because of Christ (Matt. 24: 9)
False prophets appear and deceive many (Matt. 24: 10)
The great unequaled distress on the world (Matthew 24: 21)
(S5)

(S6)(S7)

The two witnesses prophesy for 1260 days, they turn water to blood
and strike the earth with plagues (Rev. 11:3-6)

(1)- Temple abomination of desolation Daniel 9:27, 11:31, Matthew 24:15
(2) - Those in Judea must flee to the mountains, Matthew 24:16
(3) - Gospel of the kingdom is preached to the whole world, Matthew 24:14
(4) - The end of the age, Matthew 24:14
(5) - The sun will be darkened, moon will not give its light, stars fall from the sky
     heavenly bodies will be shaken, Matthew 24:29
(6) - The sign of the Son of Man appears in heaven, every one mourns, Matthew 24:30
(7) - The Son of man comes with great power and glory and his angels gather (rapture) his elect, Matthew 24:30,31
(S5) - (S7) - The last three of the seven seals on the book of life are broken, Revelation 6
(8) - 144,00 Sealed, Christians are celebrating/worshiping in heaven, fire thrown down to the earth with thunder,
     lightening, and an earthquake, Revelation 7,8:5
(T1) - (T7) - The seven trumpet judgments, the last three are the three woes, Revelation 8,9,11:15-19
(9) - The 2 witnesses are killed, lie in the streets for 3.5 days and then are brought up to heaven

REVELATION 12

The first five verses of Revelation 12 cover a vast amount of time, but they are there to give the heavenly perspective to the final three and a half years of The Tribulation. The common understanding of these verses is that the woman is a sign which represents God's chosen people (Israel) and the crown, with the twelve stars, represents the twelve tribes of Israel. The woman is pregnant and about to give birth to the Savior of the world (Christ) who will eventually rule all the nations with a rod of iron (Psalms 2:9, Rev 2:27, 19:15).

The opposing sign is a red dragon (Rev 12:3), which represents Satan. His tail swept away a third of the stars, indicating the percentage of angels that followed Satan and became demons. The red dragon has seven heads, ten horns and on his head seven diadems (Rev 12:3). These symbols are mentioned again in Revelation 17:9-13. The seven heads may represent seven world rulers and the ten horns likely represent the ten kings that will rule immediately before the beast appears and conquers three of them as stated in Daniel 7:7, 8. This same imagery is used of the Great Harlot in Revelation 17. The symbols are explained there but since the Great Harlot and Satan are not the same, the explanation in Revelation 17 may not fully apply.

It is clear from Revelation 12:4 that Satan wanted to destroy the Christ child the moment Jesus was born. But the child is snatched up (after His earthly ministry and crucifixion) to be with God on his throne as seen by Stephen (Acts 7:55-56).

The woman fleeing into the wilderness (Rev 12:6) for three and a half years is not Mary fleeing to Egypt (note that the woman flees after her child is caught up to heaven and that she flees into the wilderness not to Egypt). The woman fleeing is Israel, she is fleeing to the mountains as described in Matthew 24:15-21. This period starts at the midpoint of The Tribulation, at the abomination of desolation referred to by Christ in Matthew 24:15 and spoken of by Daniel the prophet in Daniel 11:31.

Therefore, at the midpoint of The Tribulation, Satan, the accuser is thrown down to Earth and is no longer allowed in heaven. Satan's chief aim throughout history is to lead the world astray (Rev 12:9). When Satan is thrown down he immediately pursues Israel but Israel is spared supernaturally (Rev 12:13-16). The two wings of the great eagle are given to Israel to help her flee. Satan pours water like a river out of his mouth to attempt to sweep her away with a flood but the earth drinks up the river. Israel successfully flees to a place prepared for her (Rev 12:6). Israel most likely flees to Edom, Moab, and part of Ammon, because they are not controlled by the beast in the last three and a half years of the Tribulation (Daniel 11:41). This area is modern day Jordan. Jordan is only about 30 miles from Jerusalem, borders Israel, and is currently the only Arab nation that is truly friendly towards the nation of Israel. Once Satan is frustrated over his efforts to overtake the woman (12:15) he is enraged and turns his anger on making war with the rest of her children, namely, those that hold to the testimony of Jesus, i.e., Christians (Rev 12:17)! This is proof positive that Christians are present in the last half of The Tribulation and they are, in fact, the main adversary of Satan during that time. This should come as no surprise because of what is indicated in Daniel 7. Daniel 7 states that the beast (Satan's empowered agent) is wearing down the saints of the Highest One for the same three and a half years as described in Daniel 7:21, 25. This is the last three and a half years of The Tribulation.

It is important to note that Christians are referred to as children of the woman Israel (Rev 12:17). We are heirs of the promise and are true children of Abraham (Rom 4:16 and Gal 3:7). Christians need to remember that the ultimate victory is assured; Christ will reign as described in Daniel 7:14,18.

The beast will be even more powerful and despicable in the last three and a half years as Satan is then present and desperate. The relationship between the beast and Satan is presented in Revelation 13.

REVELATION 13

The chapter opens with the dragon standing on the shore of the sea, and a beast with ten horns and seven heads coming up out of the sea. This beast is representative of all four of the beasts in Daniel 7. This beast is like a leopard, with feet like a bear and the mouth of a lion. These animals represented the first three beasts in Daniel 7. Looking at the verses in parallel format below allows us to see where they are similar.

Daniel 7	Revelation 13
2 Daniel said, "I was looking in my vision by night, and behold, the four winds of heaven were stirring up the *great sea*. 3 And *four great beasts* were coming up from the sea, different from one another.	1 And the dragon stood on the sand of the *seashore*. Then I saw *a beast* coming up out of the sea, having *ten horns* and seven heads, and on his horns were ten diadems, and on his heads were blasphemous names.

4 The first was like a *lion* and had the wings of an eagle ... 5 And behold, another beast, a second one, resembling a *bear.* ... 6 After this I kept looking, and behold, another one, like a *leopard*	2 And the beast which I saw was like a *leopard,* and his feet were like those of a *bear,* and his mouth like the mouth of a *lion.*
which had on its back four wings of a bird; the beast also had four heads, and dominion was given to it. 7 After this I kept looking in the night visions, and behold, *a fourth beast,* dreadful and terrifying and extremely strong; and it had large iron teeth. It devoured and crushed and trampled down the remainder with its feet; and it was different from all the beasts that were before it, and it had *ten horns.*	And the dragon gave him his power and his throne and great authority. 3 I saw one of his heads as if it had been slain, and his fatal wound was healed. And the whole earth was amazed and followed after the beast; 4 they worshiped the dragon because he gave his authority to the beast; and they worshiped the beast, saying, "Who is like the beast, and who is able to wage war with him?"
8 While I was contemplating the horns, behold, another horn, a little one, came up among them, and three of the first horns were pulled out by the roots before it; and behold, this horn possessed eyes like the eyes of a man and a mouth uttering great boasts.....25 He will speak out against the Most High and wear down the saints of the highest one, and he will intend to make alterations in times and in law; and they will be given into his hand for a time, times, and half a time.	5 There was given to him a mouth speaking arrogant words and blasphemies, and authority to act for forty-two months was given to him. 6 And he opened his mouth in blasphemies against God, to blaspheme His name and His tabernacle, that is, those who dwell in heaven. 7 It was also given to him to make war with the saints and to overcome them

The beast in Revelation 13:1 has ten horns as does the fourth beast in Daniel 7:7. In Daniel 7 there is a transition to a little horn that uproots three horns and this little horn is the beast of the end times. In Revelation 13 there is no mention of a little horn but instead the beast has seven heads (Rev 13:1). These seven heads are explained in Revelation 17:10.

> "… and they are seven kings; five have fallen, one is,
> the other has not yet come; and when he comes, he
> must remain a little while." (Rev. 17:10)

At the time of John's revelation, the sixth king was present and five had fallen. The seventh king is thought to be a revived Roman empire because it "was" and "is not" (Rev 17:11). The beast is an eighth but one of the seven. This will be discussed more in Revelation 17 but from this passage it's clear this beast is the culmination of world rulers and equal to the little horn of Daniel 7. The Dragon gives his authority to the beast (Rev 13:4) and he is able to control virtually the whole world for 42 months, that is, 3.5 years. The world follows after him and also worships the Dragon (Satan) at this time. This beast blasphemes God and all who dwell in heaven and he makes war against the saints (Christians) and overcomes them (verse 7) as mentioned in Daniel 7:21, 25.

The beast becomes Satan's warring agent against Christians. The world population becomes split between those who dwell upon the earth and those written in the Lamb's book of life (verse 8). Those that dwell upon the earth are those only concerned with worldly things.

Those that are written in the book of life are destined to captivity if they are peaceful in following God, or to be killed by the sword if they are actively countering Satan and the beast (verse 10). The saints must have faith and perseverance at this horrible time. This is the last three and a half years of The Tribulation because at the end the saints receive dominion with Christ and the beast is destroyed as described in Daniel 7.

In Revelation 13:11 we see another beast coming from the earth as opposed to coming from the sea. This beast has the appearance of a lamb but his words are of Satan. At this point there are three Satanic leaders on earth.

1. The dragon (Satan himself)
2. The beast of Daniel 7,9 and 11 and Revelation 13:1-4
3. A beast with the appearance of a lamb in Revelation 13:11

I think this new beast that looks like a lamb may be a religious leader of a "Christian" church, which has fully compromised with Satan. He will deceive those in the "Christian" churches who are not written in the book of life and will cause them to worship the beast. This person can perform great signs such as bringing fire down from heaven. He deceives all those who dwell upon the earth (those not written in the book of life) and commands them to worship the beast. In verse 12 it states that the first beast had a fatal wound, which was healed. He also commands those that dwell upon the earth to create an image of the beast, which is then brought to life by his power. Any who do not worship the image of the beast are to be put to death. It is somewhat understandable that all who are not written in the book of life would be deceived by these supernatural events.

At this point the beast requires everyone who wants to buy or sell to have the mark of the beast on their right hand or their forehead (verse 17). With the technology today the mark could be an imbedded chip that would identify you and allow you access to your financial accounts, which are all totally electronic today.

The number of the beast is given as 666. What the 666 refers to has been a mystery to Christians through the ages. Most likely it is numerology of the person's name. Whatever it is, I feel it will become clear to believers who are being horribly persecuted at this time. By this prophecy fulfillment, God will re-assure Christians that He is in control of all things.

A summary of Revelation 13 is as follows:

1. It discusses the last 3.5 years of the seventieth week of Daniel. (Rev 13:5)
2. Satan is on earth empowering a world ruler, the beast. (Rev 13:4)
3. Their main goal is to persecute and overcome believers. (Rev 12:17,13:7)
4. Another person, likely a religious leader, performs great signs in support of the beast. (Rev 13:11-13)
5. An image of the beast is set up for all to worship. (Rev 13:14-15)
6. The image is made to speak and if you do not worship it, you will be put to death. (Rev 13:14-15)
7. If you want to buy or sell you must take the mark of the beast. (Rev 13:16-17)

TIMELINE 9 looks at the last 3.5 years of The Tribulation with the events through Revelation 13.

TIMELINE 9 - REVELATION 6-13 WITH THE LAST 3.5 YEARS OF MATTHEW 24 TIMELINE

Last 3.5 years of Daniel's 70th week

(1)(2)   (3)   (4)
                                                              (5)(6)(7)

Christians handed over to be persecuted and be put to death (Matt. 24:9)
Christians hated by all nations because of Christ (Matt. 24: 9)
False prophets appear and deceive many (Matt. 24: 10)
The great unequaled distress on the world (Matthew 24: 21)
                                            (S5)

The two witnesses prophesy for 1260 days, they turn water to blood
    and strike the earth with plagues (Rev. 11:3-6)
Satan thrown down to earth, makes war with Christians for 3.5 years (Rev 12:17)
Israel supernaturally protected for 3.5 years (Rev 12:6,14)
The beast and an additional beast rule the world showing great signs (Rev 13, Mt.24:24)   (S6)(S7)
    The mark of the beast is required to buy or sell (Rev 13:16-17)   (8)(T1)-(T6)
                                                                                      (9)(T7)

(1)- Temple abomination of desolation Daniel 9:27, 11:31, Matthew 24:15
(2) - Those in Judea must flee to the mountains, Matthew 24:16
(3) - Gospel of the kingdom is preached to the whole world, Matthew 24:14
(4) - The end of the age, Matthew 24:14
(5) - The sun will be darkened, moon will not give its light, stars fall from the sky
    heavenly bodies will be shaken, Matthew 24:29
(6) - The sign of the Son of Man appears in heaven, every one mourns, Matthew 24:30
(7) - The Son of man comes with great power and glory and his angels gather (rapture) his elect, Matthew 24:30,31
(S5) - (S7) - The last three of the seven seals on the book of life are broken, Revelation 6
(8) - 144,00 Sealed, Christians are celebrating/worshiping in heaven, fire thrown down to the earth with thunder,
    lightening, and an earthquake, Revelation 7,8:5
(T1) - (T7) - The seven trumpet judgments, the last three are the three woes, Revelation 8,9,11:15-19
(9) - The 2 witnesses are killed, lie in the streets for 3.5 days and then are brought up to heaven

REVELATION 14

The events of Revelation 14 are best viewed as chronologically coming after Revelation 13. This seems logical because the text, which originally had no chapter breaks, is right after it. Revelation 14 opens with the phrase "Then I looked," which gives a slight indication of a continued vision. Further, Revelation 14:9 references the mark of the beast, a topic that first appeared in 13:16-17. Therefore, at the start of Revelation 14 the state of the world is as follows;

Satan is on earth

He is persecuting Christians

He is giving his power to the beast

Christians are being killed or put into prison

You need to take the mark of the beast to buy or sell

Chapter 14 starts with a description of 144,000 people who follow the Lamb wherever He goes. This would seem to be the exact same 144,000 from Revelation 7 for the following reasons:

- The number is the exact same, 144,000
- The timing of their appearance is the same
  - near the end of the last 3.5 years
  - before God harms the earth, (Rev 7:3, 14:19-20)
- Both groups have a seal of God on their foreheads (Rev 7:3,14:1)

In 14:4 it states that the 144,000 are first fruits to God and to the Lamb. Every Jew would know that "first fruits" refers to the very first of the harvest, which is to be sacrificed to the Lord (see Exodus 23:16,19, 34:22,26, Leviticus 2:12, 23:10,17,20). This incredible little statement is really the only proof needed to understand that the rapture of the church (the harvest) has not happened yet, but will happen immediately following the dedication of the first fruits to the Lord. That is in fact the exact sequence that we see in Revelation chapter 7. After the 144,000 (first fruits) are sealed, there is a multitude from every nation in heaven and they have come out of the great tribulation. In Revelation 14 we see the 144,000 first fruits are with the Lamb and shortly after this, we see the Son of Man (Christ) harvests the earth, 14:14-16.

"Then I looked, and behold, a white cloud, and sitting on the cloud was one like a son of man, having a golden crown on His head and a sharp sickle in His hand. And another angel came out of the temple, crying out with a loud voice to Him who sat on the cloud, "Put in your sickle and reap, for the hour to reap has come, because the harvest of the earth is ripe." Then He who sat on the cloud swung His sickle over the earth, and the earth was reaped." (Rev 14:14-16)

This is not the first time the gathering of Christians is referred to as the harvest. Just as "first fruits" is a very common term for Jews, the term harvest is very common for Christians. There are churches that are named "Harvest" and there is the well-known Harvest Crusade run by Greg Laurie from Harvest Christian Fellowship in Riverside, California. Examples of the harvest being used for the gathering of believers can be found in;

- Matthew 13:24-30, 36-43
- Mark 4:26-29
- Luke 10:1-2

And He was saying to them, "The harvest is plentiful, but the laborers are few; therefore beseech the Lord of the harvest to send out laborers into His harvest." (Luke 10:2)

The timing of this harvest is directly after the mentioning of the 144,000, just as the scene of heaven in Revelation 7 is directly after the sealing of the 144,000. The scene of heaven in Revelation 7 is the result of the harvest described in Revelation 14:14-16.

The Three Angels
The First Angel

In Revelation 14:6 we see an angel is flying in mid heaven, bringing an eternal gospel to every tribe and nation. This is essentially the last call to worship God before the harvest of Revelation 14:14-16. This is the fulfillment of Matthew 24:14.

"This gospel of the kingdom shall be preached in the whole world as a testimony to all the nations, and then the end will come." (Matt 24:14)

"And I saw another angel flying in midheaven, having an eternal gospel to preach to those who live on the earth, and to every nation and tribe and tongue and people;" (Rev 14:6)

The passage in Matthew states that the end shall come shortly after this last call for worship of the Lord.

The Second Angel

The second angel proclaims that Babylon the Great has fallen. Babylon's fall will be discussed in Revelation 17 and 18. From a chronological point of view there are two options for the fall of Babylon:

1. At this instant Babylon has been destroyed, or
2. This is a prophetic proclamation saying that Babylon has fallen from worshipping the one true God and will be destroyed.

Option 2 is the best choice as it allows for a post rapture destruction of Babylon which is implied in Revelation 17-19.

The Third Angel

A third angel then announces the eternal future of those who worship the beast or take the number of his name (to buy and sell). They will have no rest but will be tormented with fire and brimstone. True Christians will be empowered by the Holy Spirit, will recognize the beast and will refuse to take the mark of the beast.

A Voice From Heaven

After the three angels make their proclamations, a voice from heaven announces

"Write, 'Blessed are the dead who die in the Lord from now on!'". "Yes," says the spirit, "so that they may rest from their labors, for their deeds follow with them." (Rev 14:13).

Revelation 14:13 indicates a change. Those who die in the Lord are *now* blessed. What has changed so that those who die are now treated differently? I have seen no commentaries that note the change; most just comment on the fact of the blessing. The reason for the change is simple but also shows the precision of Scripture and of the rapture moment. In 1 Thessalonians 4:15-17 it states that as Christ descends from Heaven the dead in Christ shall rise first. So, if in fact the dead in Christ rise first there will be some small amount of time in which if you die after the dead are raised, but before the rapture, you (not just your soul) will be immediately taken to Christ. This is the change!

Immediately after the voice from heaven declaring the change for those that die in the Lord, the Son of Man (Christ), who has appeared on a white cloud, harvests (verse 16) the Christians. It is surprising to me how few people think that this harvest is the rapture of believers. This point in time is the same point in time as Matthew 24:31 and Revelation 7.

"And He will send forth His angels with a great trumpet and they will gather together His elect from the four winds, from one end of the sky to the other." (Matt 24:31).

Matthew 24:31 is the only verse where Christ mentions a rapture like event. From Revelation 7 it is clearly a world-wide rapture of tribulation believers prior to the harming of the earth by the trumpets.

Immediately following the harvest of Revelation 14:16, it is stated, that the grapes of wrath are ripe, indicating that God's wrath and judgment of the earth will begin. This is exactly the sequence that is described in Revelation chapter 7 and 8 and therefore supports that Revelation 7:9-17 is the result of the harvest (rapture) of Revelation 14:16:

- The 144,000 are sealed prior to harming the earth.
- The Christians are seen in heaven coming out of The Tribulation.
- The Lord's harming the earth begins in Revelation 8.

This of course means that the last seals should line up with the events of Revelation 13. The fifth seal is representative of Christian martyrdom, which is certainly a theme of Revelation 13.

Combining the passages so far, the detailed timeline of the rapture moment could be as follows:

- Severe martyrdom of Christians (Dan 7:21,25; Matt 24:9; Rev 6:9-11,13:10,15).
- The 144,00 first fruits are sealed and are with Christ (Rev 7:3-8, Rev 14:1-5).
- The eternal gospel is preached to all nations, (Rev 14:6, Matt 24:14).

- The sun and moon will not give its light and the stars will fall (Matt 24:29; Rev 6:12-13).

- Christ will descend from Heaven (1 Thess 4:16-17).

- The dead in Christ rise first (1 Thess 4:16-17).

- For a short time, those who die immediately go to be with Lord, bodily not just their soul (Rev 14:13).

- The son of man comes on the clouds (Matt 24:30; Rev 14:14).

- Christ gathers (harvests) his elect (Matt 24:31; Rev 14:14-16).

- There is celebration and worship of the Lord in Heaven (Rev 7:9-17).

- God's wrath begins as fire comes down from heaven and the trumpet judgments begin (Rev 8:1-7, 14:18-20).

Revelation 14 is concluded in verse 20, which states that the result of the wine press of the wrath of God is blood up to the height of the horse's bridles (5 feet) for a distance of two hundred miles. This occurs outside the city of Jerusalem. Verse 20 is likely a summary statement of what is to follow. It likely represents the results of the battle of Armageddon, which is described as bowl of wrath (plague) six, in Revelation 16.

REVELATION 15 AND 16

Revelation 15

The events described in Revelation 15 chronologically follow the events of Revelation 14. The events of Revelation 15 events are at the same time as the events described in Revelation 7:9-17. This chapter describes the martyred Christians, who are victorious over the beast, worshiping God and the Lamb (Christ) in heaven. This confirms that the martyrdom of the Christians in Revelation 13 has ended and the harvest of Revelation 14 was indeed the rapture of the church as now the Christians are in heaven.

Immediately after the above scene, seven angels with seven plagues are introduced. These angles come out of the temple and they are given seven bowls of wrath. The seven angels are of a clean, bright color indicating a righteous judgment. No one is permitted to enter the temple until the seven plagues of the seven angels are finished. It is unknown to me as to why that is, except to note that all Christians have been raptured and the only believers on earth are the 144,000 Jews first seen in Revelation 7. At this time there also would still be the two witnesses guarding the temple from Revelation chapter 11.

Revelation 16

Revelation 16 describes the seven bowls of wrath (plagues). The timing of the bowls of wrath is exactly the same as the seven trumpets in Revelation 8. These events occur after the martyrdom (seal five in Rev 6:9-11 and Rev 13:7-10,15) and directly after a scene in heaven (Rev 7 and Rev 15) with raptured Christians. The trumpets and the bowls are possibly different symbols describing the same events, but from a different perspective. The bowls of wrath can be summarized as follows:

1. Bowl 1 - Loathsome and malignant sore
2. Bowl 2 - Sea becomes blood, everything in it dies
3. Bowl 3 - Rivers and springs like blood
4. Bowl 4 - Sun scorches man with fierce heat
   a. Men blaspheme God and do not repent
5. Bowl 5 - Beast's kingdom darkened, men gnaw their tongues
   a. They blaspheme God and do not repent
6. Bowl 6 - Euphrates dries up, kings from east come for the battle of Armageddon. Three unclean spirits perform signs and gather the kings of the earth for the battle
7. Bowl 7 - Announces "it is done"
   a. Flashes of lightening and sounds of thunder
   b. A great earthquake, Jerusalem split into three parts great cities fall, islands disappear and mountains are not found
   c. Babylon comes under God's wrath
   d. Huge hailstorm, hail weighing a hundred pounds!
   e. Men blaspheme God

The trumpets are summarized as follows;

1. Trumpet 1 - Hail and fire hurled to earth,
   $\frac{1}{3}$ of the earth burns
2. Trumpet 2 - Huge mountain of fire into sea,
   $\frac{1}{3}$ of sea to blood
3. Trumpet 3 - Great fiery star falls on the rivers,
   $\frac{1}{3}$ of rivers turn bitter, and many die from it
4. Trumpet 4 - A third of the stars, moon and sun grow dark, a third of the day and night have no light
5. Trumpet 5 - (Woe 1) Smoke darkens the earth and locusts from the smoke torment man so he longs to die
6. Trumpet 6 - (Woe 2) Four angels at the Euphrates
   a. An Army of 200,000,000 appears
   b. A third of mankind are killed by the smoke, fire, and brimstone
   c. Mankind does not repent of their evil
7. Trumpet 7 - (Woe 3) Mystery of God finished (from Rev 10:7)
   a. The temple is opened
   b. Flashes of lightening and sounds of thunder
   c. A great earthquake
   d. A great hailstorm

Clearly there are differences between the above lists but the similarities are also very striking. The arguments for them being the same or overlapping are as follows:

1. They happen at the same time, right after the rapture.
2. Trumpet 2 and Bowl 2 are similar judgments of the sea.

3. Trumpet 3 and Bowl 3 are similar judgments of the rivers.

4. Trumpet 5 and Bowl 5 are darkening of the earth and great pain.

5. Trumpet 6 and Bowl 6 are great battles where the nations gather. Both involve the Euphrates river

6. Trumpet 7 and Bowl 7 are very similar in their finality and the lightening, thunder, earthquakes, and hailstorm.

7. The temple is filled with smoke and no one is able to enter until the Bowls are finished (Rev 15:8) and when Trumpet 7 sounds the temple is opened.

Although there are differences, there is also a somewhat convincing argument that they are the same events being described differently with different signs. At a minimum, it is clear that the time period of Trumpet 7 and Bowl 7 must be overlapping for each one to declare it is the end.

Revelation 16 wraps up a consecutive narrative that began with Revelation 12. Both Revelation 11 (the seventh trumpet) and Revelation 16 end with the completion of the judgment.

TIMELINE 10 looks at the very last part of The Tribulation starting with the sealing of the 144,000 including the events through Revelation 16.

TIMELINE 10 - REVELATION 6-16, DETAILING OUT THE VERY END

	Millenium

(3)

(4)
(5) (6) (7)
(S6) (S7)
(8) (9) (T1),(T2), (T3),(T4), (T5) (T6) (10) (T7)
The two witnesses are still supernaturally active
(11)(12)(13)
(B1),(B2), (B3),(B4), (B5) (B6) (B7)

(1) - Not shown
(2) - Not shown
(3) - Gospel of the kingdom is preached to the whole world, Matthew 24:14
(4) - The end of the age, Matthew 24:14
(5) - The sun darkened, moon will not give its light, stars fall heavenly bodies will be shaken, Matthew 24:29
(6) - The sign of the Son of Man appears in heaven, every one mourns, Matthew 24:30
(7) - The Son of man comes with great power and glory and his angels gather his elect, Matthew 24:30,31
(S6) - (S7) - The last two of the seven seals on the book of life are broken, Revelation 6
(8) - 144,00 Sealed as first fruits, Revelation 7, 14:1-4
(9) - Christians are celebrating/worshiping in heaven, fire thrown down to the earth with thunder, lightening, and an earthquake, Revelation 7,8:5, Revelation 15:2-4
(T1) - (T7) - The seven trumpet judgments, the last three are the three woes, Revelation 8,9,11:15-19
(10) - The 2 witnesses are killed, lie in the streets for 3.5 days and then are brought up to heaven, Rev 11:9-12
(11) - The dead rise first, in gap before rapture the dead go directly to heaven, 1 Thess. 4:14-17, Revelation 14:13
(12) - Son of Man harvests the earth, Revelation 14:15-16, the same event as (7) = the rapture
(13) - The grapes of God's wrath are harvested, his judgments will begin, Revelation 14:18-19
(B1) - (B7) - The seven bowls (plagues) of judgment, Revelation 16

REVELATION 17 AND 18

Revelation 17 and 18 go together and describe the destruction of the mysterious Babylon. There are many clues given about the identities of the various characters in the plot but unfortunately a complete and precise explanation is never given.

Revelation 17

To understand Revelation 17 it is important to separate out all the characters and write down their attributes as given in the text. The characters and their attributes as mentioned are:

The Harlot = woman on the beast = Babylon the Great = the great city

- sits on many waters = many people, nations and tongues (17:1,15).
- commits acts of immorality with kings of the earth (17:2).
- clothed and adorned richly (17:4).
- the mother of harlots and abominations (17:5).
- martyrs the saints and witnesses of Jesus (17:6).

- the woman sits on seven mountains (17:9).
- is the great city which rules over the kings of the earth (17:18).

Kings of the earth

- commit acts of immorality with Babylon (17:2).

The beast on whom the Harlot sits = the eighth king = the beast of Revelation 13

- has blasphemous names (17:3).
- has 7 heads (17:3) which are:
    - 7 mountains on which the harlot sits (17:9).
    - 7 kings (17:10).
- has 10 horns (17:3).
- was, is not, and will come out of the abyss and go to destruction (17:8).
- an eighth king and one of the seven kings (17:11).
- hate the Harlot, make her desolate, burn her up with fire (17:16).

Seven kings

- five have fallen (17:10) xxxxx, xxxxx, Babylon, Media Persia, Greece.
- one is (17:10), Rome,
- one future king (likely the Harlot).

Ten Kings

- receive authority at the time of the beast, for a short time (17:12).

- they give their power and authority to the beast (17:13).

- they wage war against the Lamb (17:14).

- hate the Harlot, make her desolate, burn her up with fire (17:16).

The above facts make it clear that at the time of the beast there is a great world power, the one future king, and that must be the Harlot. The Harlot clearly rules over many nations of different languages and is depicted as riding the beast at the beginning of the chapter (17:1). For the beast to become the eighth world dominant king he must overcome the Harlot.

It is clear from Revelation 17:16 that the beast hates the Harlot and will conquer the Harlot, burning her up with fire. This conflict with the beast clearly does not mean that the Harlot is good because the Harlot is the mother of harlotry and abominations and is drunk with the blood of the saints (17:6).

The fact that the woman sits on seven mountains (17:9) has been a topic of much speculation. It has been said that Rome was built on seven hills and therefore the rebirth of the Roman kingdom could be in play. Also, because the Vatican is in Rome, the Pope is always a target. But the beast is the head of the reborn Roman kingdom as can be seen in Daniel 9:27, where the people of the beast who is to come destroy the city and the sanctuary. This occurred in 70 AD and was done by the Roman kingdom. It is stated that the beast, the eighth king, was one of the seven and Rome is the sixth king so that fits. The fact that the woman sits on the seven hills may be showing that she is ruling over the seven hills and not a physical location. This would make sense just as the woman is riding the beast shows that she has authority over the beast at that time.

The discussion of the seven kings on which the woman sits is not fully resolved in my mind. Assuming that the phrase "five have fallen, one is and the other has not yet come" (Rev. 17:10) is true at the time of the writing, then the sixth king is Rome. This would be true for any of the dates given for the writing of Revelation, assuming the kings relate to kingdoms and not individuals, except in the case of the beast. Given the information in Daniel 2, 7, and 8 one can speculate the following:

- king 3 is Babylon.
- king 4 is Media Persia.
- king 5 is Greece.

Verse 10 states that five kings have fallen and the 6th king is currently reigning. Rome was the reigning kingdom when Revelation was written and is the fourth kingdom in Daniel 2 and Daniel 7. Therefore king 1 and king 2 must occur before Daniel's time. A reasonable guess for those two would be Egypt, and Israel during the reign of David and Solomon. A potential logical list of the 8 kings would be:

1. Egypt
2. Israel
3. Babylon
4. Media Persia

5. Greece
6. Rome
7. The Great Harlot
8. The beast

The last item to discuss is who does the Harlot represent. Revelation 18 provides many more facts about the Harlot. One thing that is clear; the Harlot is not the beast, as some have wrongly concluded, because in 17:16 it states that the beast hates the Harlot.

Revelation 18

The first step is to collect all of the facts relating to the Harlot, the mysterious Babylon. The facts are as follows:

- dwelling place of demons (18:2).
- prison of unclean spirits and every unclean and hateful bird (18:2).
- nations have drunk the wine of her immorality (18:3),
- merchants of the earth have become rich by her wealth (18:3).
- her sins have piled up as high as Heaven (18:5).
- she lived sensuously (18:7),
- she says in her heart, "I sit as a queen and will not see mourning" (18:7).
- she bought cargoes of everything including slaves (18:12-13).
- she was adorned in fine linen, gold, precious stones and pearls (18:16).

- all who had ships at sea became rich by her wealth (18:19).
- in one hour she is brought to ruin (18:10, 17, and 19).
- her merchants were the great men of the earth (18:23).
- all the nations were deceived by her sorcery (18:23).
- in her was found the blood of the prophets and of the saints and all who have been slain on the earth (18:24).

From the list above it is clear that Babylon (the Harlot) is the leading power of the world, and the most wealthy power on the earth. She imports much of the world's wealth using ships at sea. She also leads the world down a path of immorality (Hollywood and internet filth) and her business people are considered the great men of the earth (Apple, Microsoft, Walmart, McDonalds, Facebook, Boeing). The United States of America actually fits this description almost perfectly. If the end times are soon, then the USA is the only solution. If the Lord tarries another hundred years, then the mysterious Babylon could be a resurrected Babylon in the Middle East.

There are a few things in the list above that are interesting. The cargo of slaves was definitely true at one time for the USA. The blood of all the prophets and saints seems overstated for now but the country is rapidly heading to an anti-Christian, anti-Israel position. The strength of the Christian segment in the United States has gone from dominant, to barely toler-ated in the last 60 years. I think within 20 years the USA will be ready to make practicing true Christianity illegal and within 8 years will likely take away the tax-exempt status of churches that have faith based requirements for employment. In the USA common decency has been replaced by celebrated immorality. In Revelation 17:5 Babylon is called the mother of harlots. The Greek word for harlot is *porne*, which is where the word pornography comes from. Pornography literally means pictures of harlots. The USA could be called the mother of porn, because the USA is the mother of the internet which originally was mostly used for porn and even now estimates are that 35% of internet downloads are porn related.

The last thing to comment on is the timing of the destruction of Babylon. It is clearly near the end of The Tribulation period, as God is dealing out retribution for the persecution of the Saints, then Babylon will get hers. The phrase "fallen, fallen is Babylon the Great" (18:2) is the exact phrase as Revelation 14:8. The phrase in both instances could be used to describe the current moral state in the USA and also is declaring prophetically that soon her destruction will soon come. The words in 18:4 are either a warning cry, or a call to God's people to come out of Babylon as part of the rapture.

"I heard another voice from heaven, saying, "Come out of her, my people, so that you will not participate in her sins and receive of her plagues." (Rev 18:4)

It may be more likely a calling out as part of the rapture because of the timing and similarities in the sequence of Revelation 14:8-16 and Revelation 18:1-8.

Revelation 14:8-20	Revelation 18:1-19
An angel announces, "Fallen, fallen is Babylon the great." 14:8	An angel announces, "Fallen, fallen is Babylon the great." 18:1-3
Another angel declares that those who worship the beast or its image, or receive a mark on their forehead or hand will experience God's wrath. 14:9-11	Another angel calls God's people to come out of Babylon because the Lord will soon judge her. 18:4-8
The son of man wields his sharp sickle to harvest the earth. The wrath of God begins 14:14-20	Babylon's quick fall. 18:9-19

Babylon's destruction is likely part of the fire judgment of the earth that starts right before the first trumpet and includes the first trumpet (Rev 8:5-7). It may actually be a nuclear event given that the destruction is in a very short time (Rev 18:10, 17) and the merchants stand back and do not come to her aid (Rev 18:15). Also, note Revelation 17:16 which describes this destruction of the harlot as making her desolate and naked and burning her up with fire.

The other interesting note is that her destruction comes in one hour. Whether this is a literal hour, which would indicate a nuclear event or a supernatural event, it is not known. The destruction occurring in one hour may shed some light on the oft quoted Revelation 3:10 where it says that the church of Philadelphia will be kept from the hour of testing that will come upon the whole earth. Assuming that Revelation 3:10 is prophetic, the hour of testing could relate to the hour of Babylon's destruction.

REVELATION 19

Revelation 19 is a continuation of events from Revelation 18 describing the celebration of the destruction of Babylon. In Revelation 19:1 John hears a great multitude in heaven. Hence, this is clearly post rapture. The multitude is the raptured Christians because they are referred to as bond servants (Rev 19:5). This great multitude is celebrating and worshipping God, proclaiming that his judgments are true and righteous. They are also proclaiming that the destruction of Babylon was justified and avenged the blood of his bond servants (Christians).

The marriage of the Lamb to the church is the next event on the calendar. This marriage occurs after Babylon is destroyed but before Christ conquers the beast in Revelation 19:20. Revelation 19:5-8 is the first passage that refers to the bond servants as the bride of Christ but the wedding/wedding feast analogy has been presented twice in Matthew.

Matthew 22:1-14 describes the kingdom of Heaven as compared to a king who gave a wedding feast for his son. The king has his servants gather the guests from the street, but if they do not have the right wedding clothes (white robes I would expect) they are thrown into the outer darkness.

Matthew 25:1-13 gives a parable of ten virgins. Five virgins are left out of the wedding feast because they are unprepared and must go and buy additional oil for lamps. Meanwhile the other five virgins that were prepared ahead of time with additional oil are able to go into the wedding feast.

Revelation 19:8 states that the bond servants are dressed in fine linen that is clean and bright. This is consistent with other passages in Revelation were the Christians who are known as the overcomers will be dressed in white (Rev 3:4, 5, 18, Rev 6:11, Rev 7:9).

In Revelation 19:11-15 someone called Faithful and True comes on the scene riding a white horse. In righteousness he will judge and wage war. He has a new name written on Him, which no one knows. Christ must be the one riding the horse because the rider is referred to as the Word of God, the same phrase that John (the writer of Revelation) used in his gospel to refer to Christ (John 1:1, 14). His eyes are a flame of fire just as Christ's are in Revelation 2:18. It is also clear that the rider is Christ, because in verse 15 it says He is the one who will rule the nations with a rod of iron (see Rev 2:27, 12:5). In verse 15 the rider is described as having a sword coming from his mouth. This description was used of Christ in Revelation 1:16, 2:12, and 2:16.

Christ is on the scene to finish the judgment of the beast and the earth. Revelation 19:19 matches up directly with bowl six of Revelation 16:12-16. This is when all the armies of the world gather to battle God in the Battle of Armageddon. It does not seem to be an evenly matched battle because in the next verse the battle is already won and the beast and false prophet are seized and they are thrown alive into the lake of fire (19:20). The rest of the armies of the world are killed with the sword which comes from Christ's mouth. Christ is now ready to reign as promised in Daniel 7:27 and Revelation 11:17.

REVELATION 20

In the beginning of Revelation 20 an angel binds Satan for a thousand years. This is the thousand-year period known as the millennium. Satan is thrown into an abyss and can not deceive the nations, but is allowed to come out after a thousand years. Those who are part of the first resurrection come to life and reign with Christ for a thousand years. These facts seem fairly clear especially given the context of immediately following Revelation 19. However, different positions about the millennium (1,000 years) have been developed.

Premillennial

This position comes from the natural flow of the text in Revelation19 and 20. Premillennialists believe that at the end of the seven year tribulation period Satan is sent to the abyss and held for a 1,000 years while Christians rule on earth with Christ. Satan comes out one last time to deceive the nations and they gather for battle against the Lord's people but fire comes down from heaven and devours them. The devil is thrown into the lake of fire, and all the dead (those not written in the book of life) are judged and thrown into the lake of fire. A new heaven and a new earth are set up for God's people and the new earth is illumined by God.

Amillennial

Amillennialists believe that the millennium started at either Christ's resurrection or on the day of Pentecost when the disciples received the Holy Spirit, and that Christ is ruling today from heaven through the Christians on earth. Satan is bound and cannot deceive the nations. The 1,000 year period is figurative and represents the perfect completion of Christ's rule. For C.S. Lewis fans this is represented in *The Lion, the Witch and the Wardrobe* when Aslan leaves Peter, Susan, Edmund, and Lucy. They are left wearing crowns symbolizing their rule over the realm until Aslan returns.

I prefer the Premillennial position for the following four reasons;

1. Daniel 7 is quite specific about the sequence

- A terrifying final kingdom will arise (Rome) (Dan 7:7).
- Ten kings will arise out of that kingdom (Dan 7:7,24).
- Another king will arise and subdue three kings (Dan 7:8).
- He will be opposed to Christ and Christians (Dan 7:21).
- He will want to change times and laws (Dan 7:25).
- Christians will be in his hand for a time, times and half a time (Dan 7:25).
- The heavenly court will sit for judgment (Dan 7:26).

- The beast's dominion is taken away and destroyed forever (Dan 7:26).
- The dominion of all kingdoms is given to Christ and his saints (Dan 7:14,18,27).

2. There is a strong Jewish belief that when the Messiah comes there is a golden age on earth. This has not come true yet. This golden age is supported by texts in Isaiah.

Isaiah 2:1-4

- Nations will seek truth from the house of the Lord.
- Swords hammered into plowshares.
- A nation will not lift up swords against another nation.

Isaiah 11:1-10

- The Messiah will rule in righteousness.
- He will strike with the rod of his mouth.
- The wolf will dwell with the lamb.
- The leopard will lie down with the goat etc.
- The lion will eat straw like an ox.
- A child will put his hand on the viper's den without consequence.
- The earth will be full of the knowledge of the Lord.

3. There are many promises that Christians will reign in the future. Most of these promises were written well after Pentecost and were referencing a future time.

- The meek shall inherit the earth (Matt 5:5).
- Christians will reign in the future (2 Tim 2:11-12).
- Christians will rule over nations in the future (Rev 2:26-27).
- Christ's purchased followers will reign on the earth (Rev 5:9-10)

4. Amillennialism has an optimistic view that as the earth is evangelized a golden age will begin. After 2000 years, the golden age still does not seem imminent. Instead it seems to be just the opposite as life on earth spirals down as in Matthew 24:12 where it says in the end, most people's love will grow cold because of lawlessness.

There is also a question about who is reigning with Christ. Revelation 20:4 could be interpreted in the NIV to state that only the beheaded reign with Christ for a thousand years. The NASB and ESV does not make the beheaded an exclusive group because the "and those" in verse 4 could be interpreted as an additional people group not just an additional description of the beheaded. Even with those translations it seems that it could be just the resurrected believers from The Tribulation that are ruling. I feel the interpretation that only the beheaded are to reign is inconsistent with the rest of the Bible where it states that Christians will reign on the earth such as:

- Saints are given dominion (Dan 7:27).
- Christians will reign in the future (2 Tim 2:11-12).
- Christians will rule over nations in the future (Rev 2:26-27).
- Christ's purchased followers will reign on the earth (Rev 5:9-10).

It would also be inconsistent with 1 Thessalonians 4:16-18 which implies the resurrection of all believers before the rapture. In summary, it is likely that all believers reign with Christ for 1,000 years.

The plain reading of the text indicates, for reasons only known by God, that the 1,000 years of Christ's rule will end with Satan being released to deceive the nations one last time. The nations gather around Jerusalem for battle but they are destroyed by fire from heaven. The devil is finished off and thrown into the lake of fire. The devil, the beast, and the false prophet, which is the second beast, are tormented in the lake of fire forever. The concept that Satan rules over eternal hell is wrong as the text clearly states that he is tormented there forever as well.

The Great White Throne Judgment

The dead are now before the throne for judgment. The question is who are these dead? All believers were resurrected prior to the 1,000 years according to 1 Thessalonians 4:16-18. The dead would then be anyone who died during the 1,000 years and all the prior dead who were not believers. At the judgment anyone, not found written in the book of life, is judged by their deeds and is thrown into the lake of fire, which is the second death. This final verdict should be avoided at all costs and should drive our everyday evangelism efforts.

TIMELINE 11 looks at the very last part of The Tribulation starting with the sealing of the 144,000 through the events of Revelation 20.

TIMELINE 11 - REVELATION 6-20, DETAILING OUT THE VERY END

| Millenium

(7)
(S7)
(S6)   (8) (9) (T1),(T2), (T3),(T4), (T5)   (T6)   (10) (T7)
The two witnesses are still supernaturally active
(11)(12)(13)
(B1),(B2), (B3),(B4), (B5)   (B6)   (B7)
(14)   (15)   (16)(17)   Jesus and saints rule the nations

(1) - (6) - not shown
(7) -   The Son of man comes with great power and glory and his angels gather his elect, Matthew 24:30,31
(S6) - (S7) - The last two of the seven seals on the book of life are broken, Revelation 6
(8) -   144,00 Sealed as first fruits, Revelation 7, 14:1-4
(9) -   Christians are celebrating/worshiping in heaven, fire thrown down to the earth with thunder, lightening, and an
          earthquake, Revelation 7,8:5, Revelation 15:2-4
(T1) - (T7) - The seven trumpet judgments, the last three are the three woes
(10) - The 2 witnesses are killed, lie in the streets for 3.5 days and then are brought up to heaven, Rev 11:9-12
(11) - The dead rise first, in the gap before rapture the dead go directly to heaven, 1 Thess. 4:14-17, Revelation 14:13
(12) - Son of Man harvests the earth, Revelation 14:15-16, the same event as number 7 = the rapture
(13) - The grapes of God's wrath are harvested, his judgments will begin, Revelation 14:18-19
(B1) - (B7) - The seven bowls (plagues) of judgment, Revelation 16
(14) - Babylon the harlot is destroyed by the beast, Revelation 18:8-19
(15) - The wedding of the lamb to the church, Revelation 19:7
(16) - The beast and false prophet are thrown into the lake of fire, Revelation 19:20
(17) - Satan thrown into abyss and sealed there for 1000 years, Revelation 20:1-3

REVELATION 21 AND 22

Revelation 21

After the 1,000 years, God makes everything new (Rev 21:5). There is a new heaven and a new earth. The new earth is much different than the old. The facts of the new earth are as follows:

1. There will be no seas (21:1)
2. God will dwell on the earth (21:3)
3. There is no more death, mourning, crying or pain (21:4)
4. He who overcomes inherits all of this , they are in the book of life (21:7)
5. All evil, unbelieving people are in the lake of fire (21:8)
6. The new Jerusalem is dressed in all her glory with a street of gold (21:15-21)
7. There is no temple in it (21:22)
8. Jerusalem is illumined by Christ (21:23)
9. Only those written in the book of life are allowed in (21:27)

The bride of Christ (21:9), everyone written in the book of life (21:27), lives in the new Jerusalem. It appears that during this time there are nations and kings that bring their glory into Jerusalem. These nations walk by Jerusalem's light, which must mean in spiritual obedience to God who illumines the city, as they bring their glory to Jerusalem.

Revelation 22

The final chapter concludes not only Revelation but also all Scripture for nearly 2,000 years. The first part of Revelation 22 is a conclusion of the vision of the new heaven and the new earth. The last part the chapter is to send the church into the 2,000 years of the church age.

The new earth is described as having a river of the water of life flowing down the middle of the street of gold. On either side of the river is the tree of life with 12 kinds of fruit. There is no longer any curse. This undoubtedly refers to the curse given after Adam ate of the forbidden fruit in Genesis 3:14-19. Presumably on the new earth toil is not required to reap the harvest of the earth. It is repeated that there is no night because God illumines those in heaven.

The final words starting in Revelation 22:10 are interesting especially because Christ indicates that the time is near and therefore the words of the prophecy are not to be sealed up. This is the opposite of Daniel 12:9 where he is told the words are sealed up until the end of time. The combination of verses that says he is coming quickly and the time is near are striking given that there has now been over 1,900 years of waiting.

- Behold I am coming quickly (22:7).

- Blessed is he who heeds this prophecy (22:7).

- The time is near (22:10).

- Behold I am coming quickly (22:12).

- Yes I am coming quickly (22:20).

As stated early on, none of these verses say his return is imminent, but they are nonetheless troubling. The only solution is that for God, 1,000 years is as a day (2 Pet 3:8) and that, individually, our death will quickly bring the end, because when Christians die their souls go to heaven, but they sleep and then awake just prior to the rapture. Christians are to be ready for his return like the five virgins who brought oil (Matt 25:10). Christ followers need to thirst after the spiritual water of life, which is free (Rev 22:17).

Clearly Revelation 22:18 is a warning that Revelation and therefore the Bible should not have parts added or taken away. If someone adds to the Scripture the plagues will be added unto him, if someone takes away from the book, then his part in the tree of life will be taken away. This last book in the Bible is the only one that contains such a warning.

CLOSING THOUGHTS

The point of prophecy, in the Bible, is the building up of the body of Christ. The Bible is the only book that contains specific predictive prophecy that accurately tells the future. Prophecy coming true provides assurance to believers that no event is outside of God's control.

God's people have been called to suffer, sometimes extremely, throughout the church age. Believers must be spiritually ready to suffer whatever God calls them to, and remain staunch in their belief that God is in control of all things. I realize that many people will retain a pre-trib rapture position after reading this book. My sincere hope, for them, is that this book creates an awareness of another position on the timing of the rapture. So that, if the rapture is late in The Tribulation and the church is called to suffer through the breaking of the seals for Christ, they will not lose heart but remain confident that God is in control.

APPENDIX 1

Summary Listing of Events in Chronological Order
Early events

The Messiah will be cut off and have nothing
(Dan 9:26)

The destruction of Jerusalem by Rome
(Dan 9:26, Matt 24:34)

The weakening and transition of Rome
(Dan 2:40-43, 7:24)

Prophetic markers of the end times

Jews back in the Holy Land and technology exists
and supplies exist for a rapid building of the
temple (Dan 11:31, Rev 11:1)

People go back and forth and knowledge increases
(Dan 12:4)

The technology widely exists for the world to view
the two dead prophets (Rev 11:9)

Population growth to support a 200 million-man
army from the East (Rev 9:16)

Technology exists for the beast to stop buying and
selling unless the mark of the beast is taken
(Rev 13:17)

The rise and fulfillment of the Mysterious Harlot -
Babylon (Rev 17 & 18)

Events immediately prior to The Tribulation

The rise of ten kings (Dan 2:42-44, 7:24, Rev 17:12)

The rise of the prince who is to come, the beast,
a descendant of the Roman Empire
(Dan 7:24, 9:26, 11:22-23)

The beast practices deception and gains power
(Dan 11:22-26)

The beast pulls 3 of the ten kings out by the roots
(Dan 7:8)

There are wars and rumors of wars
(Dan 7:24, 11:21-26, Matt.24:6)

Negotiations on a holy covenant between the beast
and the many (Dan 9:27)

Covenant Signed – The Tribulation Starts

The temple is being rebuilt (Dan 11:31, Rev 11:1)

The heavenly court sits for judgment (Rev 4 and 5)

Jesus begins to open the seals on the book of life
(Dan 7:10; Rev 6:1)

Seal 1 - The beast, appearing as good, goes out
conquering (Rev. 6:2)

Seal 2 - Continuing war between the beast and
other kings (Dan 11:28-30, Matt 24:7, Rev 6:4)

The beast shows regard for those who forsake the
covenant (Dan 11:30)

Seal 3 - Famine (Matt 24:7, Rev 6:5-6)

Midpoint of The Tribulation

Satan is thrown out of Heaven (Rev 12:9)

The beast displays himself in the temple = the abomination of desolation (Dan 11:31, Matt 24:15, 2 Thess 2:3-4)

The sacrifices in the temple are stopped (Dan 9:27, 11:31)

Primarily Jewish believers in Jerusalem/Israel flee to the wilderness/Jordan (Matt 24:16, Rev 12:6, Dan 11:41)

The beginning of the Great tribulation (Matt 24:21)

The two prophets start to protect the temple (Rev 11:1-3)

The great persecution of Christians begins (Dan 7:25, Matt 24:9, Rev 12:17)

The beast speaks out against the most high, magnifies himself (Dan 7:25, 11:36, Rev 13:5)

The beast attempts to alter time (Dan 7:25)

The beast persecutes Christians (Dan 7:25, 12:7, Rev 13:7)

Seal 4 - Death reigns over 1/4 of the earth (Rev 6:8)

Those that dwell upon the earth (TTDUTE) worship the beast (Rev 13:8)

Those that have insight give understanding to the many (Dan 11:33)

Beast 2 arrives on the scene (Rev 13:11)

Beast 2 is a false Christ (Rev 13:11, Matt 24:24)

Beast 2 performs great signs (Matt 24:11,24, Rev 13:13)

Image of beast 1 is made and comes to life
(Rev 13:15)

Must have the mark of the beast to buy or sell
(Rev 13:16)

Terrible time of distress (Dan 12:1)

Seal 5 - martyred saints cry out from heaven
(Rev 6:11)

Seal 6 - There is a great earthquake, the sun
becomes black, moon like blood, stars fall, sky
split apart, mountains and islands move, great
men of the earth hide (Matt 24:29, Rev 6:12-16)

144,000 sealed, first fruits of the harvest
(Rev 7:3-4, 14:1-4)

The gospel is declared to the whole world by an
angel (Matt 24:14, Rev 14:6-7)

Seal 7 is broken allowing the Book of Life to be
opened

The dead in Christ are raised (Dan 12:2,
1 Thess 4:16)

For some small amount of time when Christians
die but before the rapture they go directly
to heaven (Rev 14:13)

Christ descends on a cloud (Matt 24:30, Rev 14:14)

Rapture (all verses are simultaneous)

Those written in the book of life are rescued
(Dan 12:2)

Christ's angels gather together the elect
(Matt 24:31)

Those who are left are caught up in the clouds to
be with the Lord forever (1 Thess 4:17)

The son of man harvests the earth (Rev 14:15-16)

God's people are called out of Babylon (Rev 18:4-5)

Post Rapture

Those from The Tribulation are in heaven dressed
in white (Rev 7:9-17)

They are singing the song of the Lamb (Rev 15:2-4)

The Wrath of God Poured Out

After seal 7 there is silence in heaven for ½ an hour
(Rev 8:1)

Seven angels with 7 trumpets stand before God
(Rev 8:2)

Fire is thrown down on the earth, perhaps on the
Harlot Babylon (Rev 8:5, Luke 12:49)
(Rev 17:16,18:8)

Trumpet 1 - Hail and fire hurled to earth, $\frac{1}{3}$ of
the earth burns (Rev 8:7), perhaps the Harlot
Babylon

Bowl 1 - Loathsome and malignant sore (Rev 16:2)

Trumpet 2 - Huge mountain of fire into the sea, $\frac{1}{3}$ of
sea to blood (Rev 8:8)

Bowl 2 - Sea becomes blood, everything in it dies
(Rev 16:3)

Trumpet 3 - Great fiery star falls on the rivers, $\frac{1}{3}$ of
rivers turn bitter, and many die from it (Rev 8:10)

Bowl 3 - Rivers and springs like blood (Rev 16:4)

Trumpet 4 - A third of the stars, moon and sun grow dark a third of the day and night have no light (Rev 8:12)

Bowl 4 - Sun scorches man with fierce heat. Men blaspheme God and do not repent (Rev 16:8)

Trumpet 5 - (Woe 1) Smoke darkens the earth and locusts from the smoke torment man so he longs to die. They are tormented for five months. (Rev 9:1-11)

Bowl 5 - Beast's kingdom darkened, men gnaw their tongues. They blaspheme God and do not repent. (Rev 16:10)

The marriage of the lamb (Rev 19:7-9, could be earlier)

Christ (Faithful and True) rides out with armies of heaven to strike down the nations. (Rev 19:11-19)

Trumpet 6 - (Woe 2) Four angels at the Euphrates. An Army of 200,000,000 appears. A third of mankind is killed by the smoke, fire, and brimstone. Mankind does not repent of their evil (Rev 9:13-21)

Bowl 6 - Euphrates dries up, kings from east come for the battle of Armageddon. Three unclean spirits perform signs and gather the kings of the earth for the battle. (Rev 16:12-16)

The two prophets, who have been guarding the temple, are killed by the beast. (Rev 11:7)

They lie in the street viewed by the world (Rev 11:9)

Those on the earth celebrate the death of the two prophets (Rev 11:10)

After 3 and 1/2 days the two prophets are brought to life and raised into heaven (Rev 11:11-12)

Trumpet 7 - (Woe 3) Mystery of God as quoted in Rev 10:7 is finished. The temple is opened. Flashes of lightening and sounds of thunder, a great earthquake and a great hailstorm all occur. (Rev 11:15-19)

Bowl 7 - Announced "it is done". Flashes of lightening and sounds of thunder, a great earthquake, Jerusalem split into three parts, great cities fall, islands disappear and mountains are not found (Rev 16:17-21)

The beast and the false prophet are thrown into the Lake of Fire (Dan 7:11,26, Rev 19:20)

Satan is thrown into the abyss.
(Dan 9:27, Rev 20:2-3)

The Millennium and On

Christians rule with Christ for 1,000 years
(Dan 7:14, 27, Rev 20:4)

The Messiah will rule in righteousness. He will strike with the rod of his mouth. The wolf will dwell with the lamb, the leopard will lie down with the goat, the lion will eat straw like an ox, a child can safely put his hand on the vipers den, and the earth will be full of the knowledge of the Lord (Isaiah 11:1-10)

Satan is released after a 1,000 years for the final deception (Rev 20:7-9)

Satan is thrown into the Lake of Fire (Rev 20:10)

The Great White Throne judgment (Rev 20:11-15)

New heaven and new earth (Rev 21:1)

God is on the earth (Rev 21:3-4)

The bride of the Lamb dwells there (Rev 21:9)

There is a new Jerusalem (Rev 21:10-21)

There is no sun or moon, the earth is illumined by
God. (Rev 21:22-23)

Notes on the sequence:

1. The chronological order is presented as the trumpets
    and bowls being the same or overlapping, but there
    is admittedly limited evidence to support it except for
    the similarity of some of the events and the way both
    trumpet seven and bowl seven seem to declare the end.

2. The Marriage of the lamb is hard to pinpoint but it needs
    to be after Babylon is destroyed but before Christ rides
    out on the white horse to strike down the nations.

APPENDIX 2

Timelines

The timelines from 1 to 11 are compiled on the following pages for easy reference and comparison. Timeline 12 has been added as an attempt to put an overall timeline on a single page. The exact sequence of events is often directly stated in the Biblical texts but sometimes there is some judgment that needs to be applied. One such case is the wedding between the church and Christ. From Revelation 19, it is clearly after Babylon is destroyed and before Christ conquers the beast. The exact location on the timeline for this event is uncertain.

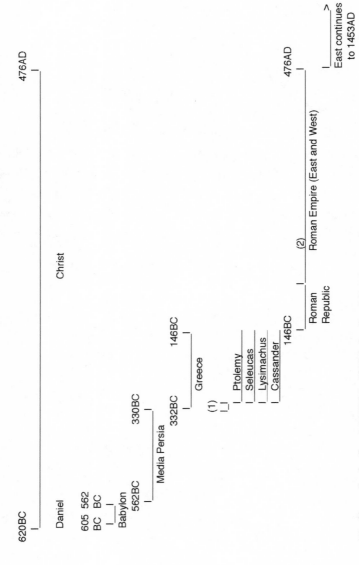

TIMELINE 1 - KINGDOM TIMELINE FOR DANIEL 2 & 7

(1) - Alexander the Great, 332BC to 323BC, the Greek kingdom was then
split into four kingdoms

(2) - Rome destroys Jerusalem in 70AD

TIMELINE 2 - DANIEL CHAPTER 2 & 7 TIMELINE OF FUTURE THINGS

(1)(2)(3)

(4)(5)

(6)

The books are opened to be reviewed by the court, one has seven seals (Dan. 7:10,Rev 5:1)

The beast is very boastful (Dan. 7:8,11)

For 3.5 years the beast shatters the power of the saints (Dan.7:21,25)

Everlasting kingdom with Christ and saints ruling (Dan. 2:44, 7:18, 22, 27)

(1) - Ten kings arise out of Rome, some strong, some brittle, Daniel 2:42, 7:24
(2) - Little horn (beast) arises, Daniel 7:8,24
(3) - Beast conquers 3 kings, Dan 7:8
(4) - Thrones are set up in preparation for judgment court, Daniel 7:9
(5) - Heavenly court sits for judgment, Daniel 7:10,26
(6) - Beast thrown into the lake of fire, Daniel 7:11,9:27, Revelation 19:20

TIMELINE 3 - DANIEL'S 70 WEEKS, DANIEL 9:24-27

* The calculation is 69 weeks * 7 yrs * 360 days/365 days = 476.4 years

GAP - an undetermined amount of time between the first 69 weeks and the final week (7 years)

(1) - Messiah the Prince is cut off and has nothing, Daniel 9:26

(2) - People of the prince (beast) destroy Jerusalem, Daniel 9:26

(3) - Daniel's 70th week = to 7 years, Daniel 9:27

(4) - Firm covenant signed between the beast and many start the last 7 years, Daniel 9:27

(5) - Sacrifice is stopped by the beast in the middle of the week, Daniel 9:27

(6) - Beast thrown into the lake of fire, Daniel 7:11,9:27, Revelation 19:20

TIMELINE 4 - DANIEL CHAPTER 2, 7 & 9 TIMELINE OF FUTURE THINGS

Daniel's 70th week = 7 years

(1)(2)(3)(4)

(5)(6)

(7)

(8)

The books are opened to be reviewed by the court, one has seven seals (Dan. 7:10, Rev 5:1)

The beast is very boastful (Dan. 7:8,11)

For 3.5 years the beast shatters the power of the saints (Dan.7:21,25)

Everlasting kingdom with Christ and saints ruling (Dan. 2:44, 7:18, 22, 27)

(1) - Ten kings arise out of Rome, some strong, some brittle, Daniel 2:42, 7:24
(2) - Little horn (beast) arises, Daniel 7:8,24
(3) - Beast conquers 3 kings, Dan 7:8
(4) - Firm covenant is signed between the beast and many for 7 years, starts Daniel's 70th week, Daniel 9:27
(5) - Thrones are set up in preparation for judgment court, Daniel 7:9
(6) - Heavenly court sits for judgment, Daniel 7:10,26
(7) - Sacrifice stopped, temple abomination of desolation, Daniel 9:27
(8) - Beast thrown into the lake of fire, Daniel 7:11,9:27, Revelation 19:20

151

TIMELINE 5 - DANIEL CHAPTER 2, 7, 9, 11 & 12 TIMELINE OF FUTURE THINGS

Daniel's 70th week = 7 years

(1)(2)(3)(4)

(5)(6) (7) (8) (9) (10)

The books are opened to be reviewed by the court, one has seven seals (Dan. 7:10, Rev 5:1)

The beast fights the king of the south

The ships of Kittim come against him
(Dan. 11:25-30)

For 3.5 years the beast shatters the power
of the saints (Dan.7:21,25)

Those who have insight (Christians) give
understanding to the many (Dan. 11:33)

They (Jews) fall by sword, flame ,captivity
and plunder (Dan. 11:33)

The king does as he pleases, he exalts
and magnifies himself (Dan 11:36)

Edom, Moab, part of Ammon are a safe
haven (Dan. 11:41)

Everlasting
kingdom
(Dan. 2:44,
7:18, 22, 27)

(1) - Ten kings arise out of Rome, some strong, some brittle, Daniel 2:42, 7:24

(2) - Little horn (beast) arises, Daniel 7:8,24

(3) - Beast conquers 3 kings, Dan 7:8

(4) - Firm covenant is signed between the beast and many for 7 years, starts Daniel's 70th week, Daniel 9:27

(5) - Thrones are set up in preparation for judgment court, Daniel 7:9

(6) - Heavenly court sits for judgment, Daniel 7:10,26

(7) - King (beast) becomes enraged at the covenant, Daniel 11:30

(8) - Sacrifice stopped, temple abomination of desolation, Daniel 9:27, 11:31

(9) - Everyone written in the book (of life) is rescued, dead raised, Daniel 12:1,2

(10) - Beast thrown into the lake of fire, Daniel 7:11,9:27, Revelation 19:20

TIMELINE 6 - MATTHEW 24 TIMELINE

Daniel's 70th week = 7 years

(1)(2)　　　　　　　　　　　　　　　　(3)　　　　(4)
　　　　　　　　　　　　　　　　　　　　　　　(5) (6) (7)

False Messiahs (vs 5)
Wars, rumors of wars (vs 6)
Nation will rise against nation (vs 7)
Kingdom against kingdom (vs 7)
Famines and earthquakes (vs 7)

Christians handed over to be persecuted and put to death (vs 9)
Christians hated by all nations because of Christ (vs 9)
Many turn away from faith, betray one another (vs 10)
False prophets appear and deceive many (vs 11)
Wickedness increases, love grows cold (vs 12)

The great unequaled distress on the world (vs 21)
False prophets perform great signs (vs 24)

(1) - Temple abomination of desolation Daniel 9:27, 11:31, Matthew 24:15
(2) - Those in Judea must flee to the mountains, Matthew 24:16
(3) - Gospel of the kingdom is preached to the whole world, Matthew 24:14
(4) - The end of the age, Matthew 24:14
(5) - The sun will be darkened, moon will not give its light, stars fall from the sky, heavenly bodies will be shaken, Matthew 24:29
(6) - The sign of the Son of Man appears in heaven, every one mourns, Matthew 24:30
(7) - The Son of man comes with great power and glory and his angels gather (rapture) his elect, Matthew 24:30,31

153

TIMELINE 7 - REVELATION 4, 5, & 6 WITH THE MATTHEW 24 TIMELINE

Daniel's 70th week = 7 years

(1)(2) (3) (4) (5) (6) (7)

False Messiahs (Mt.24:5)
Wars, rumors of wars (Mt.24:6)
Nation will rise against nation (Mt:24:7)
Kingdom against kingdom (Mt.24:7)
Famines and earthquakes (Mt.24:7)

Christians handed over to be persecuted and
put to death (Mt.24:9)
Christians hated by all nations due to Christ (Mt.24:9)
Many turn away from faith, betray one another (Mt.24:9)
False prophets appear and deceive many (Mt.24:10)
Wickedness increases, love grows cold (Mt.24:12)

The great unequaled distress on the world (Mt.24:21)
False prophets perform great signs (Mt.24:24)

(8) (S1) (S2) (S3) (S4) (S5) (S6)

(1) - Temple abomination of desolation Daniel 9:27, 11:31, Matthew 24:15
(2) - Those in Judea must flee to the mountains, Matthew 24:16
(3) - Gospel of the kingdom is preached to the whole world, Matthew 24:14
(4) - The end of the age, Matthew 24:14
(5) - The sun will be darkened, moon will not give its light, stars fall from the sky heavenly bodies will be shaken, Matthew 24:29
(6) - The sign of the Son of Man appears in heaven, every one mourns, Matthew 24:30
(7) - The Son of man comes with great power and glory and his angels gather (rapture) his elect, Matthew 24:30,31
(8) - God is seated on his throne in heaven, and the 24 elders are on their thrones, Revelation 4:2-4
(S1) - (S6) - The first six seals on the book of life are broken by Christ, Revelation 6

154

TIMELINE 8 - REVELATION 6-11 WITH THE LAST 3.5 YEARS OF MATTHEW 24 TIMELINE

Last 3.5 years of Daniel's 70th week

(1)(2)

(3)   (4)
(5)(6)(7)

Christians handed over to be persecuted and be put to death (Matt. 24:9)
Christians hated by all nations because of Christ (Matt. 24: 9)
False prophets appear and deceive many (Matt. 24: 10)
The great unequaled distress on the world (Matthew 24: 21)
(S5)

The two witnesses prophesy for 1260 days, they turn water to blood
and strike the earth with plagues (Rev. 11:3-6)

(S6)(S7)
(8)(T1)-(T6)
(9)(T7)

(1)- Temple abomination of desolation Daniel 9:27, 11:31, Matthew 24:15
(2)- Those in Judea must flee to the mountains, Matthew 24:16
(3)- Gospel of the kingdom is preached to the whole world, Matthew 24:14
(4)- The end of the age, Matthew 24:14
(5)- The sun will be darkened, moon will not give its light, stars fall from the sky
    heavenly bodies will be shaken, Matthew 24:29
(6)- The sign of the Son of Man appears in heaven, every one mourns, Matthew 24:30
(7)- The Son of man comes with great power and glory and his angels gather (rapture) his elect, Matthew 24:30,31
(S5) - (S7) - The last three of the seven seals on the book of life are broken, Revelation 6
(8)- 144,00 Sealed, Christians are celebrating/worshiping in heaven, fire thrown down to the earth with thunder,
    lightening, and an earthquake, Revelation 7,8:5
(T1) - (T7) - The seven trumpet judgments, the last three are the three woes, Revelation 8,9,11:15-19
(9)- The 2 witnesses are killed, lie in the streets for 3.5 days and then are brought up to heaven

155

TIMELINE 9 - REVELATION 6-13 WITH THE LAST 3.5 YEARS OF MATTHEW 24 TIMELINE

Last 3.5 years of Daniel's 70th week

(1)(2)

(3) (4)

(5)(6)(7)

(S6)(S7)

(8)(T1)-(T6)

(9)(T7)

Christians handed over to be persecuted and be put to death (Matt. 24:9)
Christians hated by all nations because of Christ (Matt. 24: 9)
False prophets appear and deceive many (Matt. 24: 10)
The great unequaled distress on the world (Matthew 24: 21)

(S5)

The two witnesses prophesy for 1260 days, they turn water to blood
and strike the earth with plagues (Rev. 11:3-6)
Satan thrown down to earth, makes war with Christians for 3.5 years (Rev 12:17)
Israel supernaturally protected for 3.5 years (Rev 12:6,14)
The beast and an additional beast rule the world showing great signs (Rev 13, Mt.24:24)
The mark of the beast is required to buy or sell (Rev 13:16-17)

(1)- Temple abomination of desolation Daniel 9:27, 11:31, Matthew 24:15
(2)- Those in Judea must flee to the mountains, Matthew 24:16
(3)- Gospel of the kingdom is preached to the whole world, Matthew 24:14
(4)- The end of the age, Matthew 24:14
(5)- The sun will be darkened, moon will not give its light, stars fall from the sky
heavenly bodies will be shaken, Matthew 24:29
(6)- The sign of the Son of Man appears in heaven, every one mourns, Matthew 24:30
(7)- The Son of man comes with great power and glory and his angels gather (rapture) his elect, Matthew 24:30,31
(S5) - (S7) - The last three of the seven seals on the book of life are broken, Revelation 6
(8)- 144,00 Sealed, Christians are celebrating/worshiping in heaven, fire thrown down to the earth with thunder,
lightening, and an earthquake, Revelation 7,8:5
(T1) - (T7) - The seven trumpet judgments, the last three are the three woes, Revelation 8,9,11:15-19
(9)- The 2 witnesses are killed, lie in the streets for 3.5 days and then are brought up to heaven

TIMELINE 10 - REVELATION 6-16, DETAILING OUT THE VERY END

Millenium

```
(3)
        (4)
  (5)  (6)  (7)
(S6)        (S7)
        (8)  (9) (T1),(T2), (T3),(T4), (T5)          (T6)
        The two witnesses are still supernaturally active          (10)  (T7)
                (11)(12)(13)
                (B1),(B2), (B3),(B4), (B5)      (B6)          (B7)
```

(1) -   Not shown
(2) -   Not shown
(3) -   Gospel of the kingdom is preached to the whole world, Matthew 24:14
(4) -   The end of the age, Matthew 24:14
(5) -   The sun darkened, moon will not give its light, stars fall heavenly bodies will be shaken, Matthew 24:29
(6) -   The sign of the Son of Man appears in heaven, every one mourns, Matthew 24:30
(7) -   The Son of man comes with great power and glory and his angels gather his elect, Matthew 24:30,31
(S6) - (S7) - The last two of the seven seals on the book of life are broken, Revelation 6
(8) -   144,00 Sealed as first fruits, Revelation 7, 14:1-4
(9) -   Christians are celebrating/worshiping in heaven, fire thrown down to the earth with thunder, lightening, and an
          earthquake, Revelation 7,8:5, Revelation 15:2-4
(T1) - (T7) - The seven trumpet judgments, the last three are the three woes, Revelation 8,9,11:15-19
(10) - The 2 witnesses are killed, lie in the streets for 3.5 days and then are brought up to heaven, Rev 11:9-12
(11) - The dead rise first, in gap before rapture the dead go directly to heaven, 1 Thess. 4:14-17, Revelation 14:13
(12) - Son of Man harvests the earth, Revelation 14:15-16, the same event as (7) = the rapture
(13) - The grapes of God's wrath are harvested, his judgments will begin, Revelation 14:18-19
(B1) - (B7) - The seven bowls (plagues) of judgment, Revelation 16

TIMELINE 11 - REVELATION 6-20, DETAILING OUT THE VERY END

		Millenium

(7)

(S7)

(S6)   (8)   (9) (T1),(T2), (T3),(T4), (T5)   (T6)

The two witnesses are still supernaturally active   (10)   (T7)

(11)(12)(13)

(B1),(B2), (B3),(B4), (B5)   (B6)   (B7)

(14)   (15)   (16)(17)   Jesus and saints rule the nations

(1) - (6) - not shown

(7) -   The Son of man comes with great power and glory and his angels gather his elect, Matthew 24:30,31

(S6) - (S7) - The last two of the seven seals on the book of life are broken, Revelation 6

(8) -   144,00 Sealed as first fruits, Revelation 7, 14:1-4

(9) -   Christians are celebrating/worshiping in heaven, fire thrown down to the earth with thunder, lightening, and an earthquake, Revelation 7,8:5, Revelation 15:2-4

(T1) - (T7) - The seven trumpet judgments, the last three are the three woes

(10) - The 2 witnesses are killed, lie in the streets for 3.5 days and then are brought up to heaven, Rev 11:9-12

(11) - The dead rise first, in the gap before rapture the dead go directly to heaven, 1 Thess. 4:14-17, Revelation 14:13

(12) - Son of Man harvests the earth, Revelation 14:15-16, the same event as number 7 = the rapture

(13) - The grapes of God's wrath are harvested, his judgments will begin, Revelation 14:18-19

(B1) - (B7) - The seven bowls (plagues) of judgment, Revelation 16

(14) - Babylon the harlot is destroyed by the beast, Revelation 18:8-19

(15) - The wedding of the lamb to the church, Revelation 19:7

(16) - The beast and false prophet are thrown into the lake of fire, Revelation 19:20

(17) - Satan thrown into abyss and sealed there for 1000 years, Revelation 20:1-3

TIMELINE 12 - SUMMARY TIME LINE

Daniel's 70th week = 7 years

(1)
(2)
(3)
(4)(5)(6)(7) (8) (9)

False Messiahs (Mt.24:5)
Wars, rumors of wars (Mt.24:6)

Famines and earthquakes (Mt.24:7)

(S1) (S2) (S3) (S4)

Christians are martyred (Mt.24:9)
Beast and dragon wage war on the saints (Dan. 7, Rev 13)
Christians hated by all nations due to Christ (Mt.24:9)
False prophets perform great signs (Mt.24:24, Rev. 13)
The greatest distress on the world (Mt.24:21)
The two witnesses prophesy (Rev.11)
Must have the mark of the beast to buy or sell (Rev 13:16-18)
(S5)   (S6)(S7)

(T1) - (T7)
(B1) - (B7)

(1) - Ten kings arise from Roman kingdom, beast arises and conquers 3 Kings, Dan 7:23-24
(2) - Beast makes a holy covenant for 7 years, starting Daniels 70th week, Daniel 9:24-27
(3) - In the middle of the week the Abomination of Desolation is set up, sacrifice stopped, Dan. 9:27,11:31, Matt. 24:15
(4) - 144,000 Jews are sealed to go through the time of the harming of the earth, Revelation 7:3
(5) - Saints are raptured, Daniel 12:1, Matthew 24:31, Revelation 7:9,17,14:14-16
(6) - Babylon judged, Revelation 18:8
(7) - Wedding of the Lamb, Revelation 19:7
(8) - Two witnesses resurrected, Revelation 11:11-12
(9) - Beasts into the Lake of Fire and Satan is Locked in the abyss for 1000 years, Revelation 19:20-20:3

S1-S7 - The seven seals (of the book of life) broken, Revelation 6 and 8:1
T1-T7 - The seven trumpets are blown, Revelation 8:1-9:21, 11:15-19
B1-B7 - the seven bowls are poured out on the earth, Revelation 16

APPENDIX 3

Summary of the Argument Against a Pre-Trib Rapture Pre-Trib Rapture Position

1. In Daniel 12:1-2 Daniel writes of the fate of those written in the book. Those who are alive will be rescued and those already dead will awake to everlasting life. This rapture moment is clearly well after the midpoint of the tribulation spoken of in Daniel 11:31.

2. In Matthew 24:31 the angels gather the elect after the midpoint of The Tribulation (Daniel 11:31) referenced by Christ in Matthew 24:15. This is the only gathering of the elect that is mentioned in the gospels except its companion verse in Mark 13:27. If Christ knew about an earlier rapture he kept it a secret.

3. In 2 Thessalonians 1:6-8 Paul states that Christ rescues us and deals out retribution when he comes. These two events are linked together without a 7 year gap for The Tribulation.

4. In 2 Thessalonians 2:1-4 Paul states that believers should not be deceived regarding the gathering of the church. It will not come before the man of lawlessness (the beast) is revealed and he takes his place in the temple at the midpoint of The Tribulation. Therefore, the church is not gathered (raptured) until some point after the midpoint of The Tribulation.

5. In the heavenly court descriptions in Revelation 4 & 5, just prior to the start of the breaking of the seals, there is no church present.

6. The book in Revelation 5 that can only be opened by Christ has seven seals. The best logical explanation is that the book is the book of life. The book must be opened to reveal who is to be saved per Daniel 12:1. The rapture can not occur until the 7th seal is broken allowing the book of life to be opened. The seals events described in Revelation 6 are clearly in The Tribulation period.

7. The 5th seal shows the souls of martyred Christians before the throne of God, they are told to wait a while longer before the Lord will avenge their blood. No transformed, raptured Christians seem present, only souls.

8. After the 6th seal 144,000 Jews are sealed. They are the first fruits to Christ per Revelation 14:4. The first fruits are those taken before the full harvest. These first fruits must then logically come before the harvest of Christians. The harvest comes shortly after in Revelation 14:16 and Christians are worshipping as the result of the harvest can be seen in Revelation 7:9-17 and Revelation 15:2-4, right after the 144,000 are sealed (as first fruits) in Revelation 7:3-8.

9. In Revelation 18:4, God calls his people out of Babylon before it is destroyed. This may be a reference to the rapture, and is clearly late in The Tribulation period.

10. The timing of Daniel 12:1-2, Matthew 24:31, II Thessalonians 1:6-8, 2:1-4, Revelation 6:17-7:17, Revelation 14:1-16 all easily line up to a post 6th or 7th seal rapture/harvest. A rapture of the elect at this point in The Tribulation is beyond debate. The pre-trib rapture position necessitates an additional rapture at the start

of the 7 year tribulation. This additional rapture is never discussed in scripture.

11. There is no verse in scripture that directly supports a pre-trib rapture just prior or at the start of Daniel's 70th week (The Tribulation). The arguments for a pre-trib rapture are more logical arguments from a man's perspective, not direct teachings from scripture. Three arguments for a pre-trib rapture are:

A) Christians escape the wrath of God (1 Thess 1:10,5:9); therefore they must escape The Tribulation.

B) Christ's return is imminent (can come at any time) therefore the rapture must come before The Tribulation starts.

C) Revelation 3:10 indicates that the church of Philadelphia is kept from the hour of testing that is coming on the world. Therefore, the entire church is raptured prior to the seven-year tribulation.

The argument against Point A:

Christians escape the wrath of God (1 Thess 1:10,5:9); therefore they must escape The Tribulation.

Nowhere in scripture does it state that God's wrath starts at the beginning of the 7 year tribulation period. Actually, the coming wrath of the Lord is announced at the end of seal 6 (Rev 6:16,17). Right after the sixth seal the 144,000 are sealed for their protection before the earth is harmed and then believers from The Tribulation are seen in heaven in Revelation 7. God's wrath is poured out in Revelation 8 with the trumpet judgments. The same sequence is seen in a later vision of John. In Revelation 14, the 144,000 first fruits are mentioned, then the harvest of the earth by the Son of Man, then the harvest of the grapes of wrath. Believers are then seen in heaven in Revelation 15 and God's wrath is poured out in Revelation 16 with the bowl judgments.

The argument against Point B:

Christ's return is imminent (can come at any time) therefore the rapture must come before The Tribulation starts.

First of all scripture never says that Christ's return is imminent or can come at any time. Second, for this to be true when scripture was written, Christ's return would have to be imminent before the fall of Jerusalem in 70 AD and before the fall of Rome centuries later. This would directly contradict the timing of the setup of the eternal kingdom in Daniel 2:44 and the fall of Jerusalem in Daniel 9:27. If you believe that the rapture is immediately prior to the tribulation, the following prophecies must be fulfilled before Christ's return is imminent;

- The destruction of Jerusalem by Rome (Dan 9:26, Matt. 24:34)
- The weakening and transition of Rome (Dan 2:42-44, 7:24)
- Population growth to support a 200-million-man army from the East (Rev 9:16)
- Jews are back in the Holy Land and technology exists and supplies exist for a rapid building of the temple (Dan 11:31, Rev 11:1)

- People go back and forth and knowledge increases (Dan 12:4)

- The technology created for the world to view the two dead prophets (Rev 11:9)

- Technology exists for the beast to stop buying and selling unless the mark of the beast is taken (Rev 13:17)

- The rise and fulfillment of the Mysterious Harlot - Babylon (Rev 17 & 18)

- The rise of ten kings (Dan 2:42-44, 7:24, Rev 17:12)

- The rise of the prince who is to come, the beast, a descendant of the Roman Empire (Dan 7:24, 9:26, 11:22-23)

- The beast practices deception and gains power (Dan 11:22-26)

Third, when Christ is asked in Matthew 24:3 about the signs of his return, he does not say he could come at anytime, but rather he gives many signs that would precede his coming.

The arguments against Point C:

Revelation 3:10 indicates that the church of Philadelphia is kept from the hour of testing that is coming on the world. Therefore, the entire church is raptured prior to the seven-year tribulation.

There is no scripture that states that the church at Philadelphia represents the entire church, just prior to the rapture.

There is no scripture that states the hour of testing is the equivalent of the seven-year tribulation. There are various hours discussed during The Tribulation, the hour of God's judgment in Revelation 14:6-7 would be one to consider. This hour is announced after the mentioning of the 144,000 and just prior to the harvesting of the earth by the son of man in Revelation 14:14-16.

There is no proof that God's action of keeping the church at Philadelphia from the hour of testing is accomplished by the rapture.

Therefore, this verse in isolation provides no support for a pre-trib rapture.

APPENDIX 4

Daniel 8 Musings

I currently do not include Daniel 8 in my study. The reason is primarily to reduce the length of time to get through the study. The other reason is that the church's standard position on this passage is different than mine and that necessitates a longer explanation than warranted for the limited additional information that is obtained. That being said, I will offer my position on the passage for completeness.

The main issue for me is, of course, the timing of the events in Daniel 8. The standard position of the church is that this passage is prophetically discussing the events around 169 BC, when Antiochus IV Epiphanes comes into Jerusalem and desecrates the temple and stops the sacrifice. This position has the following logic supporting it.

The ram and the shaggy goat are interpreted for us in verses 20 and 21. The ram with the two horns is Media and Persia. The shaggy goat is Greece (Alexander the Great) and that kingdom is broken into four kingdoms. This breakup occurred around 323 BC.

"In the latter period of their rule, when the transgressors have run their course, a king will arise, insolent and skilled in intrigue." (verse 23) This verse logically implies that it is describing Antiochus IV. Antiochus IV eventually took over one of the four kingdoms.

Antiochus IV magnified himself and stopped the regular sacrifice and set up an abomination in the temple fulfilling (verse 11).

The above three points certainly makes a case for Antiochus IV Epiphanes. The problem is that he does not completely and accurately fulfill the complete prophecy. My position throughout this book is that God is in control and true prophecy must be completely fulfilled.

Let's look closer at the passage and note all the facts in the prophecy that are not fulfilled by Antiochus,

"It grew up to the host of heaven and caused some of the host and some of the stars to fall to the earth" (verse 10)

For 2300 evening and mornings, then the holy place will be properly restored. (verse 14)

The vision pertains to the time of the end. (verses 17,19)

"When the transgressors have run their course." (verse 23)

"He will even oppose the Prince of princes, but he will be broken without human agency." (verse 25)

One item on the above list that eliminates Antiochus from consideration is actually repeated twice. Whenever the Bible repeats itself, it is for important emphasis, so we should pay attention to it. The Bible states clearly in verse 17 and 19 that the vision pertains to the time of the end. It is very difficult to argue that 169 BC is the time of the end.

According to 1 Maccabees the 2300 evenings and mornings are not fulfilled. In the Catholic Bible, Maccabees is a book between the old and new testaments and it records events in this time period. Protestant Bibles do not contain it because protestants feel it is not inspired by the Holy Spirit. Whether you believe it is inspired by the Holy Spirit or not, it is an excellent historical document. The year numbering used in the Maccabees is per the Jewish calendar and gives an accurate time measure. Year 143 relates to 169 BC. The key verses in Book 1 of Maccabees are as follows;

> 1:20, He attacks the sanctuary in year 143 taking all the silver and gold and costly vessels

> 1:29 – 54, On the 15 day of Casleu (November/ December) in year 145 there is an abomination of desolation set up in the temple

> 4:52, In year 148 on the 25th day of Casleu they are able to sacrifice again.

The 2300 evenings and mornings could either be 1150 days or 2300 days depending on how you interpret the verse. If the evenings and mornings are counted separately then it is 1150 days. From Maccabees it is unclear when the sacrifice is stopped but it is in either in year 143 or 145. If the starting date is taken to be year 143 then you have approximately 5 years to year 148 which is 1830 to 1860 days depending on the number of extra months added in for the Jewish lunar calendar. If you assume the sacrifice is stopped in year 145, which appears most likely from the text then there are 1080 to 1110 days depending on the number of extra months added in for the Jewish lunar calendar.

Verse 10 and verse 25 of Daniel 8 seem to be way overstated for Antiochus IV Epiphanes. The Prince of princes is viewed to be a reference to Christ and it does not seem that Antiochus opposed Christ in any battle.

It might be possible to say that the transgressors had run their course (verse 23) at the time of the beast but not in 169 BC. In fact, in Daniel 9 it is stated that 70 weeks have been decreed to finish the transgression. The end of the 70th week is at the end of The Tribulation.

I think the most logical conclusion is that Antiochus IV Epiphanes is a type of the beast who is to come. The true fulfillment is the beast, who comes at the *time of the end*. He definitely battles the Prince of princes. The beast is defeated without human agency, which could not be truly said about Antiochus IV.

The jump in time, needed, to go from the Greek kingdom to the time of the end, can be accommodated by allowing verse 23 to skip over nearly 2200 years. This certainly is not clear but in my opinion it is better than trying to explain that 169 BC is the time of the end. Remember that Daniel is promised to rise again at the end of the age (Dan 12:13). There was no rapture or resurrection in 164 BC.

The above argument is to say that the complete fulfillment of Daniel 8 is a future event at the time of the end as stated in verses 17 and 19. The sacrifice is stopped at the midpoint of The Tribulation in Daniel 11:31. According to Daniel 12:11-12,the total days from that point are 1290 days – 1335 days. That would mean that the 2300 evenings and mornings should be interpreted to be 1150 days. The fact that the days are counted by evenings and mornings could give an indication as to how horrible the time is for the person counting, as he goes through the final days of The Tribulation. There is a precedent grammatically for this in Genesis 1:5, 1:8, and Deuteronomy 28:65-67.

If the above is correct, then Daniel 8:14 must be fulfilled 1150 days after the midpoint in The Tribulation when the sacrifice is stopped. When Christ returns to throw fire on the earth at the start of the trumpets, he may soon thereafter restore the holy place, which is being protected by the two witnesses in Revelation 11.

Another interesting thought is that in verse 14 the word for properly restored is literally vindicated. The word for holy place is just holy so the literal translation could be until the holy are vindicated. This could possibly refer to the saints being vindicated or proven right. If this were the case it could refer to Christ's return or some other event that vindicates the saints . It should be noted that the word for holy is commonly used alone to refer to the holy place or sanctuary, so the line of thought that is referring to holy people (saints) should be considered just a musing.

APPENDIX 5

Small Group Discussion Questions
Questions for Daniel 2

1. What do you think of the king's plan to not tell the dream he wanted interpreted?

2. What are the arguments against the position that Christ's kingdom is already here?

3. The rise of the ten toes remains to be seen. Can we watch for that as a sign or do you think that God will not give us understanding until the beast appears?

4. Do you agree that there is no scriptural basis for an imminent return of Christ? Could he have returned while the Roman kingdom was unified and powerful? Can he return before the 10 kings are in place?

Questions for Daniel 7

1. As we (as Christians) are looking for the appearance of the beast, what does this chapter say we should look for?

2. What proof is there from this chapter that Christ's kingdom on earth is not set up yet?

3. How do the saints of the highest one fair against the beast?

4. Given that scripture will come true, what should Christians do once the beast is revealed? Note: the answer is not in this passage.

5. What was Daniel's reaction at the end of the chapter? Why?

Questions for Daniel 9

1. How can you use this passage as a witnessing tool with Jews who also hold this scripture as holy? To be prepared, think of transition questions you could use with someone to bring up this passage.

2. Given today's circumstances, what do you think might be the main points of the covenant set up by the beast?

3. At one point world opinion felt after WW II that perhaps it was the war to end all wars, as all people realized the destruction that it caused. The Bible states in verse 26 that there will be war to the end. Has world opinion or the Bible been proven correct?

4. Given what you have studied so far, what will the first 3.5 years of The Tribulation be like compared with the last 3.5 years

Questions for Daniel 10, 11, 12

1. From this section, what signs can we look for that will indicate who is the beast?

2. In Matthew 24, Christ relates that a key sign before his coming will be the abomination of desolation. What has to happen for this to take place?

3. The beast seemingly controls most the earth except for one area. Locate it on a map. How far is it from Jerusalem?

4. Do you feel that Daniel 12:1-2 represents the rapture? What are the reasons for and against? How well does it line up with 1 Thessalonians 4:13-17

5. Can you think of other examples of how Daniel 12:4 has been fulfilled.

6. What promise is given to Daniel at the end of chapter 12? Do we have the same promise?

Questions for Matthew 24

1. Can Christ return before these signs are fulfilled?

2. Can Christ's return be imminent before these signs are fulfilled?

3. Do the gospels mention another rapture other than that in Matthew 24 and Mark 13?

4. Are the seal events in Revelation 6 included in the signs in Matthew 24?

5. Verify that none of the trumpet events in Revelation 8 and 9 are mentioned as signs for Christ's return in Matthew 24.

Questions for Thessalonians

1. Who is raised first?

2. Do you believe that Christ was referring to his second coming in Luke 12:49?

3. Does it seem in 2 Thessalonians 1:6-8 that there is a gap between our relief and the Lord dealing out retribution?

4. Are you comfortable that, in the context, Paul is talking about the rapture in 2 Thessalonians 2:1-4? If so what does the warning given indicate?

5. What should be the Christian response if/when we see the beast in the temple?

Questions for Revelation 1-3

1. Does your current view of Jesus see him as a man or as described in Revelation 1?

2. What weaknesses of the seven churches are still present today? How can you impact your church to avoid the pitfalls of Revelation 2 and 3, and be over comers?

3. Make an inspirational list of all things given to those who overcome. There is one for each church. Are all of these things promised to all Christians?

4. How can you make sure you and your church are not lukewarm towards Christ?

Questions for Revelation 4-6

1. Assuming you are a Christian, are you grateful that your name is written in the Lamb's book of life? Would you weep if it could not be opened? Do you feel that the book, that only Christ can open, is the Lamb's book of life?

2. If the beast starts out on a white horse, with a crown given to him, when do you think that the discerning Christian will realize that he is the beast?

3. Seal 4 talks about the impact of wild beasts of the earth afflicting people, what are your thoughts on how this could come about?

4. Seal 5 and Daniel 7:21-25 talk about the persecution of Christians, are you ready to take a stand for Christ even if it involves severe persecution up to death?

Questions for Revelation 7

1. Why is it only necessary to seal 144,000 Jews before the earth is harmed?

2. What are your feelings about Israel still being central to God's future plans?

3. Those seen in heaven clearly had gone through tough times on earth, are you comfortable with this scenario being part of God's plan?

4. The final verse of chapter 7 shows the true intimacy that we have with God. What are your thoughts on this verse?

Questions for Revelation 8, 9, 10

1. What do you think is the significance that none of the trumpet events are given as a sign of Christ's return in Matthew 24?

2. Do you believe that Christ was referring to his second coming in Luke 12:49? Does Revelation 8 seem consistent with the events that would happen when Christ returns?
   See also 2 Thessalonians 1:6-8.

3. What do you think the reaction of the people will be as each trumpet unfolds?

4. Given the magnitude of the first four trumpets, how severe is it that the last three are much worse?

5. What do you think of the fact that no one repents in Revelation 9:20?

Questions for Revelation 11

1. Why do we know the temple exists by the mid point of Daniel's 70th week?

2. How long do you think it would take to rebuild the temple?

3. Why would the court outside the temple be given over to the nations?

4. Based on the description of the power of the two witnesses, what trumpet events in Revelation 8 & 9 could be caused by the two witnesses?

5. Why do you think they left the bodies of the witnesses in the street?

6. What is the main reason for placing the two witnesses in the second half of The Tribulation?

Questions for Revelation 12

1. Describe the heavenly scene that Stephen saw in Acts 7:56.

2. Why would we put the time that Satan is thrown down as the midpoint of the tribulation?

3. Verify where Jordan is on the map. What supernatural events help Israel flee?

4. Who becomes the main focus of Satan's wrath in the last 3.5 years? Why?

Questions for Revelation 13

1. Why is the beast so powerful?

2. What signs are performed by the beast that looks like a lamb? How convincing would these signs be?

3. At the time this prophecy was written there would be no way for someone to prevent people from buying and selling. How easy would it be today? How do you think it will be done?

4. Verify from news reports that people are already having chip implants today. Google "human chip implants".

Questions for Revelation 14

1. At this point in time what would be the predicament of someone who did not take the mark of the beast?

2. Why did John say that the 144,000 are the first fruits? If the rapture had already occurred, could he have said that?

3. Can you imagine the impact of voices from heaven being heard by everyone on earth?

4. I am confident the harvest in Revelation 14:14-16 is the gathering of believers. Can you think of anything else it could be?

5. Have you heard of the grapes of wrath before? What angel says to gather the grapes of wrath? How does this relate to Revelation 8?

Questions for Revelation 15 & 16

1. What evidence is there that the people group in chapter 15 is the same as those in chapter 7?

2. Why would you interpret the seven angels with the seven plagues to be holy and righteous?

3. Find all the similarities between the trumpets and the bowls.

4. Note the finality of the seventh bowl and seventh seal. Can the bowls follow the trumpets?

Questions for Revelation 17 & 18

1. How do we know the harlot is not the beast?

2. What happens to the harlot? Are there any indicators as to when this happens?

3. Looking up imports and exports of countries, does it seem that all who had ships at sea would ascribe their wealth to the USA?

4. Can you think of a country / kingdom other than the USA that better fulfills the list of harlot attributes in chapter 18?

5. Can verse 18:24 be said about any country / kingdom?

Questions for Revelation 19

1. If Babylon is the USA then a sign of the end being near would be the falling away of the USA from being known as a Christian nation. Is that starting to happen?

2. When on the timeline is the marriage of the Lamb to the church?

3. How long is the famous battle of Armageddon? Does God have any enemies? Can Satan be considered God's enemy if they are not somewhat peers?

4. Write down all the reasons that it is Christ who is on the white horse in verses 11-15.

Questions for Revelation 20

1. Are Christians currently reigning on earth with Christ?

2. Who rules over hell?

3. Who rules with Christ in the millennium?

4. What do we know about life in the millennium? Where do the people come from?

Questions for Revelation 21 & 22

1. What could we possibly assume about the millennium from what is listed for the new earth?

2. What are the other nations doing during this time? Are Christians ruling them?

3. Who is allowed to enter the new Jerusalem?

4. In what way is the time near as stated in Revelation 22:10?

Made in the USA
San Bernardino, CA
30 December 2018